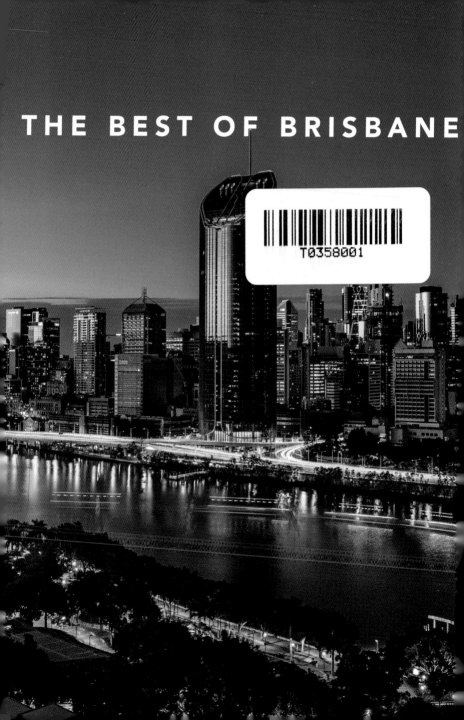

THE BEST OF BRISBANE

T0358001

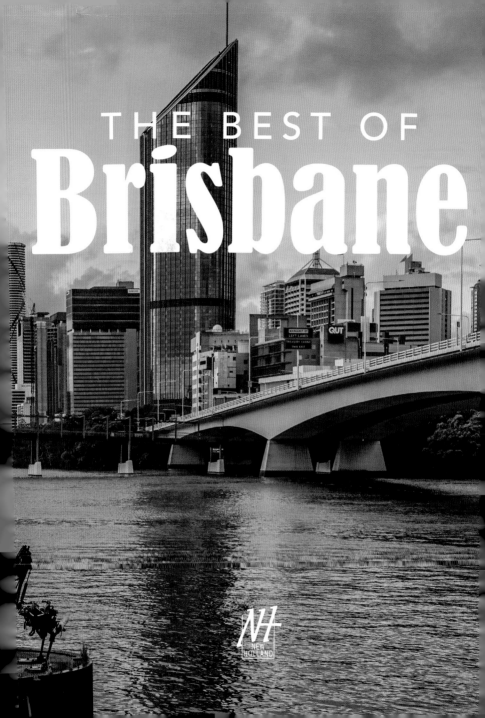

THE BEST OF
Brisbane

NEW HOLLAND

Contents

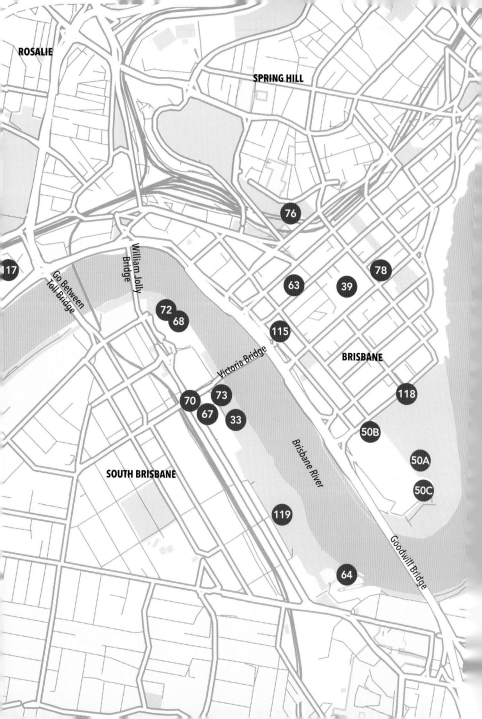

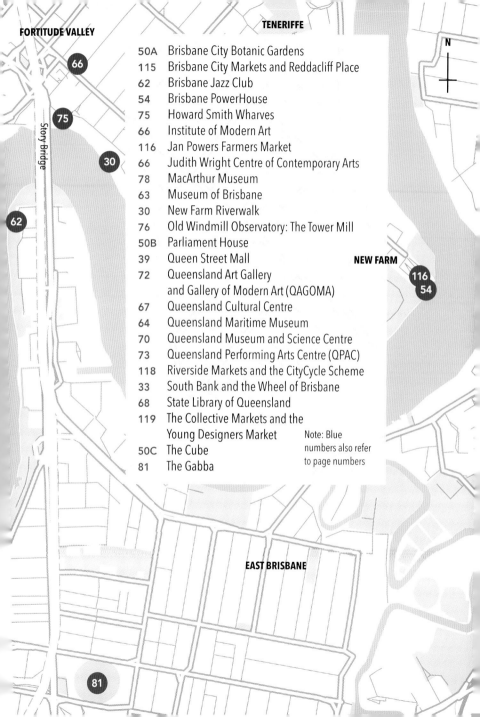

FORTITUDE VALLEY

TENERIFFE

N

Story Bridge

NEW FARM

EAST BRISBANE

Note: Blue numbers also refer to page numbers

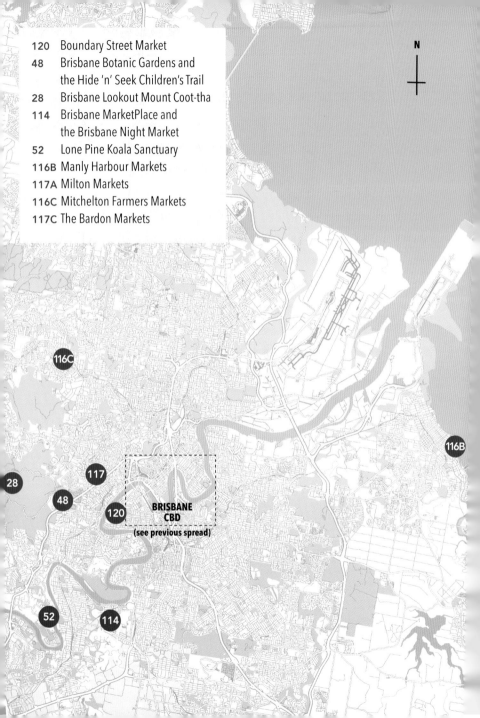

N

116C

116B

117

28

48

120

BRISBANE CBD
(see previous spread)

52

114

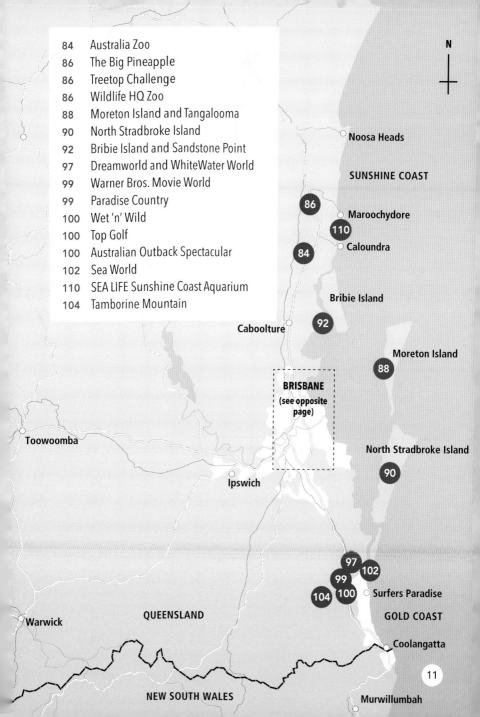

N

Noosa Heads

SUNSHINE COAST

86

Maroochydore

110

84

Caloundra

Bribie Island

Caboolture

92

Moreton Island

88

BRISBANE
(see opposite page)

Toowoomba

North Stradbroke Island

90

Ipswich

97
102
99
104 100
Surfers Paradise

QUEENSLAND

GOLD COAST

Warwick

Coolangatta

11

NEW SOUTH WALES

Murwillumbah

Welcome to Brisbane!

Brisbane is the number three city in Australia, after Sydney and Melbourne, in terms of population, but to Queenslanders and many other Australians, it's number one, combining the best of what its older and bigger sibling cities have. The capital of Queensland is situated in a goldilocks climatic zone, neither too hot nor too cold. Its European history dates from a 1799 expedition to Moreton Bay, conducted by Matthew Flinders. The potential of the area around the mouth of what was later to be called the Brisbane River was not immediately obvious.

A penal colony founded in 1824 at Redcliffe Point by John Oxley moved south due to lack of water, and when word spread about the abundant natural resources near Brisbane River the area opened up to free settlement in 1838. Governor George Gipps declared Brisbane to be a township and that it would be the capital port of the northern districts of New South Wales on 24 March 1842 – Brisbane's birthday – a fact that's known by hardly anybody. You heard it first here, folks! Brisbane was proclaimed a fully-fledged municipality on 7 September 1859.

Australians are never very far away from nature, and while Brisbane ranks behind Melbourne, Sydney, Adelaide and Perth in terms of 'livability', it's hard to see why it isn't right up there too in the global top 20. Apparently, the competition for livability at the top comes down to a fraction of a per cent. Like so many other places in Australia, Brisbane is a nice place to visit, and you *would* want to live there.

The People of Brisbane

The first human inhabitants of the region now occupied by the central business district of Brisbane were the Turrbal and Yuggera, who had been here, literally, since time immemorial. The region around the river used to be a popular meeting place for itinerant tribal groups, each one numbering in their hundreds.

Close to 2.5 million people live in Brisbane today, with 80 per cent of them being of either Australian, English, Irish, Scottish, German, Dutch or New Zealand European descent. Other notable populations include Chinese, Italian, Maori, Filipino, Samoan and Vietnamese.

Like so many Australians, Brisbanites are often immigrants, with almost a third born overseas and over half with at least one parent born overseas. Brisbane is, by Australian standards, a more genetically and culturally homogenous population, with almost 80 per cent of the population speaking only English at home.

Brisbane's Personality

In spite of having been inhabited by people for well over 50,000 years, by world standards, Australia is still considered a 'young country' and Brisbane is a young city. Brisbanites have a zesty, youthful attitude to life. There's a freshness in Brisbane and everything is in the present moment – in the 'now'.

What Brisbane Has that Other Places Don't Have

Brisbane doesn't just have a youthful *vibe*, it's demographically young too, with almost a quarter of the population being between 25 and 35 years old. This can't help but affect everything in Brisbane and when you combine it with a climate that hovers between 20° and 30° Celsius (70° to 85° Fahrenheit) in the summer and rarely dips below between 10° and 20° (50° to 70° Fahrenheit) in the winter, you have the makings of an outdoorsy city.

And there's that peaceful, meandering river too.

The city itself takes full advantage of the delights of the river and the nature that surrounds and infuses it, including **River Cruises** (page 36) a lengthy **Riverwalk** (page 30) **South Bank** (page 33) and **New Farm Park** (where all the locals like to hang out, page 54). The CBD has the nightlife of **Fortitude Valley** (page 42). Brisbane also has easy access to the wilds just a stone's throw away at **Moreton Island** (page 88) and **North Stradbroke Island** (page 90).

Please note: All opening hours, admission prices and other costs are correct at the time of publication but are subject to change without notice so, if in doubt, please telephone the venue or consult their website first.

Getting Around

Brisbane has an excellent public transport system. Ticketing is centralized through TransLink and a system called the TransLink *go* card which can be used on buses, trains, ferries and light rail not only in the city itself, but in eight metropolitan zones across south-east Queensland including the Gold Coast to the south and the Sunshine Coast to the north. As an added bonus you can also use *go* card across 11 zones in Cairns, 15 in Mackay, 11 zones in Toowoomba and 11 zones in Townsville if you plan to explore more of Queensland.

Website: **www.translink.com.au/tickets-and-fares/fares-and-zones/zones**.

You can get *go* **cards** online from **www.translink.com.au/tickets-and-fares/go-card** – or at any 7-Eleven store, G:link and busway stations, Queensland Rail stations and CityCat ferries. When using public transport, you need to tap on when you board and tap off when you arrive at your stop. If you are transferring to another service, you need to tap on again and tap off at your destination.

There is no charge for a *go* card, however the minimum value is $10 for a card balance to be used as travel credit. Concession and seniors' cards are available and you can register your travel card so that if it gets lost or stolen you can cancel it and the credit amount on the card can be transferred to a new card.

For further enquiries call **131 230**.

Maps of the Brisbane public transport network as well as all the other TransLink networks are available from most train stations or online at **www.translink.com.au/plan-your-journey/maps** and that site also has information about bus, ferry and tram services.

Brisbane's main transport hubs are Roma and Central. At Roma Street Station you'll find the Brisbane Transit Centre where you can get a lot of detailed information about getting around Brisbane – open 3.30 am to 7.00 pm seven days. One stop away to the east is Central Station on Ann Street. All references to 'How to get there' in this book use either Roma Street Station or Central as a starting reference point. To plan your trips online go to the TransLink Journey Planner: **www.jp.translink.com.au/plan-your-journey/journey-planner**.

City Centre Free Loops

The FREE City Loop and Spring Hill Loop bus services provide high-frequency public transport access within the central business district (CBD) and between the CBD and Spring Hill area, just north of the CBD.

The City Loop operates clockwise (route 40) and anti-clockwise (route 50) in both directions every 10 minutes. The routes are slightly different because of one-way streets. Distinctive red buses stop at the red signposted bus stops. Operating hours are Monday to Friday from 7.00 am to a last service that departs from Queensland University of Technology (QUT) at 6.00 pm. Stops of note include: Central Station, Botanic Gardens and Riverside.

The Spring Hill Loop (route 30) operates every 10 minutes during peak and 20 minutes during off peak. Distinctive yellow buses stop at the yellow signposted bus stops. Operating hours are Monday to Friday from 6.00 am to 6:57 pm. Stops of note include Central Station and Old Windmill Observatory. For online maps for City Loop and Spring Hill Loop just Google 'City Loop Map Brisbane'.

CityHopper

Amazingly, Brisbane also has a FREE inner-city ferry that runs every 30 minutes between 6.00 am and midnight, seven days. Its stops are: North Quay, Brisbane City – South Bank 3, South Brisbane – Maritime Museum, South Brisbane – Thornton Street, Kangaroo Point – Eagle Street Pier, Brisbane City – Holman Street, Kangaroo Point – Dockside, Kangaroo Point – Sydney Street, New Farm.

There are also a number of paid, cross-river ferries departing from Eagle Street Pier, Holman Street and Thornton Street every 10 to 15 minutes.

See: **www.brisbane.qld.gov.au/traffic-and-transport/public-transport/ citycat-and-ferry-services/cityhopper**.

Going Your Own Way

If you want to go your own way there are a number of rent-a-car companies, including all the major international chains, and yes, Brisbane also has Uber services.

Brisbane is a world-class city with a highly developed infrastructure and services, but you'll still have problems getting a cab on a Friday or Saturday night if you don't book ahead.

Brisbane Taxi Cab Numbers

Australia Wide Taxis	131 008
13cabs	132 227
Black and White	07 3255 5900
Brisbane Corporate Cars and Airport Limo Hire	1300 399 222
Delta	07 3262 9600
Independent Buranda-Yellow Cabs	07 3391 5955
Mahajan	07 3272 7849
Metropolitan	07 3892 3100
Zevra Albion	07 3262 1377

Prestige services get you a better type of limousine-style cab, when the occasion calls for it. Many cab companies offer minibus services if you need to book a cab for more than four people and can also provide baby seats or cabs that can take wheelchairs. Just let them know at the time that you book.

For **wheelchair taxis** call Brisbane Maxi Taxis on **136 294**.

In Australia, it is considered polite for at least one passenger to sit up front with the driver, unless you're only traveling as a couple. It's part of our tradition of egalitarianism, which we still pay a lot of lip service to.

Tourist Information Offices

The hubs for visitor information for Brisbane online are **www.visitbrisbane.com.au** and **www.brisbane-australia.com**.

There are several information centers within the Brisbane metropolitan area and Moreton Bay and a complete list can be found here: **www.visitbrisbane.com.au/information/visitor-essentials/visitor-information-centres**.

The main one in the city is located in **Queen Street Mall** (page 39)' **Brisbane Visitor Information and Booking Centre**

Address: 167 Queen Street, Brisbane City 4000

Phone: 07 3006 6290

Opening hours: 9.00 am to 5.30 pm Monday to Thursday, 9.00 am to 7.00 pm Friday, 9.00 am to 5.00 pm Saturday and 10.00 am to 5.00 pm Sunday.

Feel free to call on the **Brisbane Greeters** too (page 25).

The Brisbane Greeters

Brisbane has decided to do something special for visitors by establishing an initiative called Brisbane Greeters, part of the Global Greeter Network. Essentially, red-t-shirted volunteers make themselves available to visitors so that a local can show off the best that their city has to offer with stories and insights that only an insider can offer. The service is totally FREE but welcomes donations at any level of generosity.

Website: **www.visitbrisbane.com.au/brisbane-greeters**

There are several options available for groups of up to six people only:

Greeters Choice puts you entirely in the greeters more-than-capable hands and the greeter will take you on a journey discovering what your greeter loves best about Brisbane. Available at 10.00 am daily and can be booked from as little as three hours' notice.

Your Choice – Precincts can let you choose exactly where you'd like to go. Available at 10.00 am daily but you'll need to give a little more notice so that a suitable greeter is available for you.

Your Choice – Special Interests Available at 10.00 am daily, this option requires at least seven working days' notice so that a greeter can be found who shares your passions or area of interest. Current featured interests include, but are not limited to: Brisbane's Aboriginal history, German story, penal colony history, wartime history and the Walter Taylor Bridge.

Booking Guidelines: **Online booking essential** – no walk-ups accepted. The service is bookable *once* and can be experienced *once only*. Tours run for up to four hours and will try to address any special needs. Under 18s must be accompanied by an adult.

Must-Sees

Every city in Australia has a list of their must-see attractions, and while what is and isn't on a list depends on who you talk to and how long that list is, there are always a few attractions that should be on everyone's list.

Here's our list of Brisbane must-sees.

Brisbane Lookout Mount Coot-tha

Why you should go: Arguably the first thing that you should see
in Brisbane is on the fringes of the city itself. Mount Coot-tha
(Honey Mountain) acts as a backdrop to Brisbane when you're
in the city but becomes the ideal place from which to get a
panoramic view when you're there. Brisbane Lookout gives you
a sense of the breadth of the city.

Address: 1012 Sir Samuel Griffith Drive, Mount Coot-tha 4066

Website: **www.brisbanelookout.com**

How to get there: From Central take a short walk south-east to the
bus stop on the south side of Adelaide Street near the corner of

Creek Street. Catch the 471 bus and it'll take you straight there. The travel time is about 30 minutes.

Opening hours: The lookout is open 24 hours a day, 365 days a year.

Time budget: One to three hours depending on how you're getting there and how leisurely you want to take it.

How much? FREE!

While you're here: Have a snack or light meal at the **Kuta Cafe** (page 145) or a more substantial and formal lunch or dinner at the **Summit restaurant** (page 145). You can extend your day at Mount Coot-tha by visiting the **Botanic Gardens** (page 48), where you'll also find the **Mount Coot-tha Visitor Information Centre** for more information about the area.

New Farm Riverwalk

Why you should go: For an extremely pleasant stroll that gives you a feel for the city, you can't beat the Riverwalk. It's a purpose-built walkway and bicycle path bridge that goes right onto and above the river following a north-south route on the bend of the river between Kangaroo Point and East Brisbane.

Address: Starting from Boundary Street in the north and extending to Merthyr Road in the city

How to get there: From Central take a short walk south through Anzac Square until you get to Adelaide Street. Turn right (west) until you reach the bus stop on the north side of Adelaide Street for the 199 bus. Take the bus to either Adelaide Street near Boundary Street or stay on the bus a little longer until you reach Brunswick Street between Malt Street and Harcourt Street. From either of those stops it's a short stroll to the Riverwalk.

Opening hours: 24 hours a day, 365 days a year.

Time budget: About half an hour, maybe an hour if you're with small children.

How much? FREE!

While you're here: At the northern end of the walk, you're at the **Howard Smith Wharves** (page 75) so you can stroll through them before starting the Riverwalk. Continue the walk along Griffith Street and then to Merthyr Park, hug the riverbank until you turn left and north into Oxlade Drive and follow Oxlade Drive until you get to **New Farm Park** (page 54) which has, right next to it, **Jan Powers Farmers Markets** (page 116), **Brisbane Powerhouse and Powerhouse Park** (page 54). You can skip the walk up Oxdale Drive if you like and just catch the ferry one stop from the Sydney Street Wharf to the New Farm Park Wharf.

South Bank and the Wheel of Brisbane

Why you should go: South Bank is one of those examples of urban redevelopment where city planners have created a space devoted entirely to pleasure. It's busy; it's quiet. It's active; it's restful. It's big enough to accommodate a whole gamut of different moods depending on how you're feeling. Special events happen all year round. Visit the website for up-to-the-minute details.

Website: **www.visitbrisbane.com.au/south-bank/news/ the-ultimate-guide-to-visiting-south-bank**

How to get there: From Central take the train either to South Brisbane station or South Bank station. Easy! You can also take the FREE **CityHopper ferry** (page 21).

Opening hours: Southbank is open 24 hours a day, 365 days a year but individual attractions and businesses (including eateries) have their own opening hours.

Time budget: As long as you like. You could spend the whole day here.

How much? FREE! However, you can spend as much as you like in the shops and eateries.

While you're here: There's lots to experience. The list just goes on and on! There are free beaches and pools, open every day, all year round (thank you, climate of Brisbane!). Swimming highlights include **Streets Beach** – Australia's only human-made, inner-city beach, the Boat Pool and **Aquativity**, an interactive waterplay park. There are three playgrounds for the kiddies, plenty of opportunities for picnics and barbecues, walking and cycling including the kilometer-long, bougainvillea-lined Arbour Walkway, the Nepalese Pagoda and, for the foodies, the Epicurious Garden.

There's also the **Wheel of Brisbane**, the city's 60-meter-tall Ferris wheel, open 10.00 am to 10.00 pm every day.

Website: **www.thewheelofbrisbane.com.au**; adults $20.90, concessions $17.10, children $13.80, families (2 adults and 2 children 4 to 14 years) $60.80, children under 4 FREE.

The **Queensland Cultural Centre** (page 67) is immediately to the north, but you'll probably need a whole other day to spend time there. **The Gabba** (page 81) isn't far either, a four-minute bus ride on the 172 to the east.

Riverlife Brisbane River Experiences

Why you should go: Brisbane takes full advantage of its river, and there's every reason for both residents and visitors to enjoy it. Taking one of a number of rivers cruises is a lovely way to see the city – arguably perhaps the best. A number of different companies also offer Brisbane River experiences to suit your budget and interests.

Riverlife (Phone: 07 3891 5766; Website: **www.riverlife.com.au**) offers a wide range of adventure activities including kayaking, stand-up paddle boarding, abseiling, Segway and Urb-E (like mini motor scooters) tours. There are also adventure dining tours. Prices start at $39 per person up to $149 for a deluxe night dining tour.

Address: Kangaroo Point Cliffs Drive, Kangaroo Point 4169

How to get there: From Central walk south-east along Creek Street to Eagle Street Pier ferry terminal. Catch the ferry to Thornton Street ferry terminal and then walk due south, hugging the riverbank. You can't miss it. If you're fit enough to do any of the Riverlife activities then you won't mind the walk.

Time budget: At least one to two hours depending on your activity. Contact them first for a better idea of how long things take, depending on what you decide to do.

Brisbane River Cruises

Why you should go: For those who, for one reason or another, aren't quite up to the level of physical activity required for kayaking or for **stand-up paddle boarding** (page 34) and would rather that the boat do all the work, there's the option of taking a Brisbane River cruise. Two popular options from Mirimar cruises

combine a river cruise with a visit to **Lone Pine Koala Sanctuary** (page 52). The Koala Express includes a fast Brisbane River cruise to the Koala Sanctuary, takes three hours and costs from $90 per person. The longer Brisbane River Cruise and Koala Sanctuary visit takes five-and-a-half hours and costs from $80 per person on the *Mirimar II*.

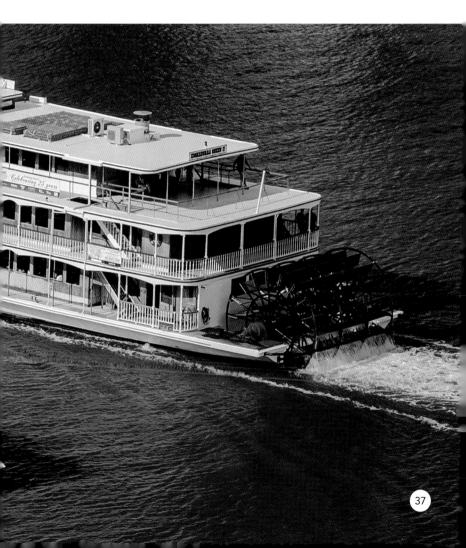

Please note: you'll need to have comfortable shoes, a hat, sunscreen and a passport or some sort of ID card. There are 28 stairs to climb from the riverbank to the entry gates at Lone Pine, so this isn't really suitable for wheelchair users.

Meeting point: Cultural Centre Pontoon on the South Bank Boardwalk, in front of QEII Park, just outside the Queensland Art Gallery near the Cultural Centre Tunnel.

Phone: 0413 749 246

Website: **www.mirimarcruises.com.au**

How to get there: Catch the train from Central to South Brisbane Station then walk north along Grey Street, turn right (east) and walk along Melbourne Street, veering north and staying north of Victoria Bridge.

While you're there: Mirimar also offers a special river cruise during the annual **Sunsuper Riverfire**, a fireworks and air show held in late September every year as part of **The Brisbane Festival** (page 126); adults $120, children (5 to 14) $70, including a two-course buffet dinner. Bookings and further information: **www.mirimarcruises.com.au/riverfire**.

Another nice option is to take a riverboat cruise on one of the Kookaburra Queens – old-fashioned paddle wheelers – and these include lunch, high tea and dinner cruises: **Kookaburra Showboat Cruises**; Phone: 07 3221 1300.

Website: **www.kookaburrariverqueens.com**.

Queen Street Mall

Why you should go: Queen Street Mall is a shopper's paradise. Containing 700 of the 1000 stores in the CBD, there's something here for practically everyone.

Address: It's a whole district centered around Queen Street, just south of Central.

How to get there: It's about a five-minute walk from Central. Stroll down (south-west) along Ann Street, turn left into Edward Street and keep going for two blocks. Or, just catch the FREE Route 50 City Loop from Central.

Opening hours: Depend on the individual businesses. Late night shopping in Brisbane is on Friday nights, when shops are open until 9.00 pm.

Time budget: 700 shops? Seriously? You could spend days here, weeks here.

Queen Street Mall connects a slew of shopping centers and arcades:

Brisbane Arcade dates from 1923 and is known for its jewelers, specialty shops like The Model Shoppe and The Tea Centre and for being the home of Brisbane fashion designers like Maiocchi, Pia du Pradal and Tengdhal.

170 Queen Street formerly Broadway on the Mall, this center leans towards homewares but also international brands like Swedish clothing retailer H&M and Japan's UNIQLO.

The Myer Centre is the biggest of them all and includes Event Cinemas and a host of other stores.

Queens Plaza, for luxury brands like Bulgari, Dior, Louis Vuitton, Yves Saint Laurent, Tiffany & Co. and a lot more.

MacArthur Central is where you go for practical stuff and it has the only full-sized supermarket in the CBD – Woolworths on the basement floor, where you'll also find BWS liquor and Priceline pharmacy.

Tattersall's Arcade dates from 1926 and has high-end clothing and accessories all on one level.

Wintergarden has a stainless steel butterfly sculpture out the front and Aquila, Oxford, Peter Jackson and a lot more.

While you're in the area: Albert Street crosses Queen Street right through the middle and offers even more shopping choices.

Fortitude Valley

Why you should go: True to the city planners' continuing vision of Brisbane as a city dedicated to sundry pleasures, Fortitude Valley, or simply 'The Valley', as it's known to locals, was Australia's first dedicated entertainment district, beginning in 1987 with the building of **Chinatown Mall**. But before that The Valley had a long and fascinating history with periods of prosperity in the 1950s and 60s to a decline into seediness from the 70s to the mid-80s. This juicy history is enshrined in dozens of heritage-listed buildings. Today, The Valley is a thriving collection of clubs, pubs, restaurants and retail shops and it always has something going on throughout the year.

Address: It's a whole suburb, just north-east of the CBD.

Website: **www.visitbrisbane.com.au/fortitude-valley**

How to get there: Take the train one stop from Central to Fortitude Valley. The trip takes all of two minutes. Easy!

Time budget: At least an hour, or all day, or all night even.

How much? FREE! At least to look around.

While you're there: The website above lists at least 30 things you can do in Fortitude Valley. There's a lot of shopping, eating and drinking to be done (especially in Chinatown), but also dancing and enjoying live music or a show at the 'The Judy' – **The Judith Wright Centre** (page 66). The more unusual things include art appreciation at the **Institute of Modern Art** (page 66), and as always, the **Brisbane Greeters** (page 25) are available to take you on a bespoke tour.

Best of Brisbane Full-Day Sightseeing Tour and Green Cabs

Sometimes you just don't have the time to invest in planning or mapping out a visit, and it's easier to let someone else make all the decisions for you. Or you might simply want an introduction to a city before you commit to a more in-depth exploration plan. In that case a viable option is to take an all-day tour. The Brisbane's Best tour run by the JPT tour group includes the following in a typical itinerary which departs from both the Gold Coast and Brisbane:

7.00 am – Departure from Gold Coast hotel

8.00 am – Departure from hotel of choice or Brisbane Transit Centre at 171 Roma Street, Brisbane at Roma Street Station

9.00 am – City sights

11.15 am – River cruise with Devonshire tea and commentary

12.00 pm – Free time at South Bank Parklands

1.10 pm to 1.25 pm – Transit to Mount Coot-tha Lookout

1.25 pm – Lookout

2:20 pm to 2.30 pm – Transit to XXXX Brewery

3.00 pm to 4.30 pm – Brewery tour

4.30 pm to 5.00 pm – Return to hotel or to Transit Centre

Phone: 1300 781 362 or 07 5630 1602

Website: **www.daytours.com.au/optional-tours/Tours/brisbanes-best**

How to get there: Roma Street Station and the Transit Centre is just one stop west of Central. Easy!

How much? Ex Brisbane Adults $139, children (3–13) $89; ex Gold Coast adults $149, children (3–13) $99, children under 3 FREE!

While you're there: Check out the range of other tours available, including tours to Australia Zoo, Lamington National Park, Gold Coast City Sights and Tangalooma.

For a more leisurely change of pace try a Green Cabs pedal cab tour from $40 for a 20-minute South Bank tour to $120 for a 70-minute Brisbane Explorer tour; Website: **www.greencabs.com.au/ tours**. Prices are *per cab* that can comfortably fit two adults.

Fun with the Kids

Because it's such a young, family-oriented city, Brisbane is probably the most child-friendly city in Australia, so there are lots of places you can take children. But some are specifically designed to appeal to the under 18s, especially if your kids are really young. Here are some places to visit that you can bring the whole family to that go the extra mile to keep the kiddies entertained.

Brisbane Botanic Gardens and the Hide 'n' Seek Children's Trail

Why you should go: Located at the east foot of Mount Coot-tha just 7 kilometers (4 miles) from the CBD the **Brisbane Botanic Gardens** are both easily accessible and offer a host of outdoorsy delights where the grown-ups can enjoy a relaxed time while the kids have 52 hectares (128 acres) to run around in. Highlights include the **Australian Rainforest**, the **Exotic Rainforest** and the **Tropical Display Dome**, the **Japanese Garden and Bonsai House** and the **Fragrant Plant and Herb Garden**.

But there's lots, lots more. Special mention to the **National Freedom Wall**, with over 16,000 dedications to those who served in World War II. At the heart of the **Exotic Rainforest** is the **Hide 'n' Seek Children's Trail**, which is like a big, fun treasure hunt.

Address: Mount Coot-tha Road, Toowong 4066

Phone: 07 3403 8888

Website: The address is a very long one. Just google
'Brisbane Botanic Garden Mt Coot-tha'.

How to get there: From Central take a short walk south-east to the bus stop on the south side of Adelaide Street near the corner of Creek Street (stop 34). Catch the 471 bus and it'll take you straight there (stop 19). The travel time is about 25 minutes.

Opening hours: 8.00 am to 6.00 pm but closes at 5.00 pm April to August.

Time budget: At least a couple of hours.

How much? FREE! At least to look around.

While you're in the area: Visit the Sir Thomas Brisbane Planetarium and the Cosmic Skydome; Phone: 07 3403 2578; Website: **www.brisbane.qld.gov.au/things-to-see-and-do/ council-venues-and-precincts/sir-thomas-brisbane-planetarium** Open from around 10.00 am to 4.00 pm Tuesday to Sunday but open until later on Fridays and Saturdays and closed on Mondays except during Queensland school holidays.

General entry is FREE but you'll need a ticket for the Skydome shows: adults $16.10, concessions $13.20, children (3–14) $9.00, family (2 adults and 2 children or 1 adult and 3 children) $44.00, children under 3 FREE!

There's also the **Mount Coot-tha Visitor Information Centre** (page 28) open from 8.00 am to 5.00 pm if you want to look at options for exploring the area further.

Brisbane City Botanic Gardens, Parliament House and The Cube

Why you should go: Brisbane's other botanic gardens are located right in the heart of the city. Opened in 1855 but dating from as early as 1828, it is now heritage-listed. It has a much more genteel and manicured feel than its younger sister at Mount Coot-tha, and at 20 hectares (49 acres) it's much smaller. But it still manages to pack quite a bit in. While it's very child-friendly, the city gardens are the place to go if you're looking for history and rarity. It's the first non-native cultivated landscape in Queensland and many of its plants are of great maturity. Key attractions are the bamboo grove, the ornamental ponds and a gorgeous river frontage. It's the perfect 'time out' place when you just want a restful, peaceful time. FREE guided discovery tours are available. If you're there in the evening from late spring to early autumn you can catch a film at the **Openair Cinema** with tickets starting at just $14.
Website: **www.openaircinemas.com.au/brisbane**

Address: 147 Alice Street, Brisbane 4000

Phone: 07 3403 8888

Website: **www.brisbane.qld.gov.au/things-to-see-and-do/
council-venues-and-precincts/parks/city-botanic-gardens**

How to get there: Route 40 of City Loop FREE buses will take you there from Central in about eight minutes.

Opening hours: Open 24 hours a day, seven days a week.

Time budget: At least an hour, longer if you're lingering for a picnic.

How much? FREE!

While you're in the area: If you're there on a Sunday go to the **Riverside Markets** (page 118). Monday to Friday you can take a peek at the nearby **Queensland Parliament** where you can see Queensland's unique version of democracy in action and go on a FREE guided tour or enjoy high tea. Phone: 1800 197 809 or 07 3553 6000; Website: **www.parliament.qld.gov.au**.

You might also take a short stroll further south to **The Cube** at the **Queensland University of Technology**. It's an amazing FREE interactive display center where the kids can have a lot of fun. Address: 2 George Street, Brisbane 4000; Website: **www.thecube.qut.edu.au**; Open 10.00 am to 4.00 pm, seven days.

Lone Pine Koala Sanctuary

Why you should go: This is the world's first and still the largest koala sanctuary so it's a must-visit for fans of the eucalyptus-munching marsupials. There's other native wildlife on show here too including platypuses. This isn't just a place to gawk, there are plenty of daily shows and activities and there are 'Premium Wildlife Experiences' available as extras too.

Address: 708 Jesmond Road, Fig Tree Pocket, 4069

Phone: 07 3378 1366

Website: **www.koala.net**

How to get there: The easiest way on public transport is to walk from Central to Adelaide Street stop 34 near Creek Street and catch bus 445 to Gunnin Street near Jesmond Road, stop 41A, Fig Tree Pocket. Total travel time including about 10 minutes walking is around 50 minutes. Arguably the better way is by **boat river cruise** that includes the price of sanctuary admission (page 36).

Opening hours: 9.00 am to 5.00 pm seven days.

Time budget: At least three hours, longer if you're taking a river cruise as well.

How much? The best place to purchase tickets is on the website. Approximate prices are: adults $38, children (3–17), pensioners, students and concessions $24, and families (2 adults and 3 children) $80, children under 3 FREE!

For the virtual visitor: The website has a link to the live koala camera where you can often catch the little darlings in a snooze cuddle. There's also a platypus camera where if you're *very* lucky you can see Australia's aquatic monotremes in action too.

While you're in the area: There really isn't anything else out here for the casual visitor, but it's pretty much an all-morning, all-afternoon or all-day trip anyway before you head back to the CBD.

New Farm Park and Brisbane PowerHouse

Why you should go: **New Farm Park** is one of the heritage-listed attractions that Brisbane has preserved to provide continuity with its past. The river-fronted park covers just over 15 hectares (37 acres) and the area was once dotted with lagoons providing rich pickings for the Indigenous inhabitants. It then became a farm (hence the name), then a racecourse before becoming a park in 1919. Today it's home to picnic and BBQ areas, a couple of tennis courts and a kids' playground.

Right next door to the east is **Brisbane PowerHouse**. As the name implies it's a former power generation station that was decommissioned in 1971 and repurposed as an arts center in 2000, with a major renovation in 2006. Besides being architecturally interesting the PowerHouse is host to all sorts of performing arts events year-round, so it's worth checking the website to see what's on offer when you visit.

Address: New Farm Park – 1042 Brunswick Street, New Farm 4005; PowerHouse – 119 Lamington Street, New Farm 4005

Phone: 07 3358 8600

Website: **www.brisbanepowerhouse.org**

How to get there: From Central catch bus 199 from stop 26 in Adelaide Street to Merthyr Road and then walk south-east (travel time about 30 minutes) *or* catch bus 196 from stop 25 on Adelaide Street to Brunswick Street at Parkview *or* catch the FREE **CityHopper ferry** (page 21).

Opening hours: New Farm Park is open all the time. The PowerHouse box office opening hours are from 9.00 to 5.00 pm Monday to Friday and 12.00 pm to 4.00 pm Saturday but performance and event times vary, so check first. The eateries are open from early till late.

Time budget: At least an hour to take a good look around and longer if you linger at PowerHouse.

How much? Performances and events prices vary.

While you're in the area: Eating at **Bar Alto** (page 135) is highly recommended. **Mary Mae's** (Phone: 07 3358 5464; Website: www.marymaes.com.au) is also on site for southern American-style food and cocktails. Just in front of the PowerHouse there's the **Jan Powers Farmers Markets** every Saturday (page 116). When you're done you can catch the ferry and continue your exploration of the river.

Story Bridge and the Adventure Climbs

Why you should go: Story Bridge is, in the popular imagination, the center of Brisbane. Its 777 meters (2549 feet) span the Brisbane River between the CBD and Kangaroo Point making access to Fortitude Valley easy. Opened in 1940, the longest cantilever bridge in Australia now carries almost 100,000 vehicles every day including bicycles and it has pedestrian access too. The road that spans the bridge is called the Bradfield Highway, which is also the name of the entirely different Bradfield Highway that spans the Sydney Harbour Bridge (although both roads were named after Dr John Jacob 'Job' Crew Bradfield). Story Bridge itself was named after John Douglas Story, who lobbied hard for its creation.

Besides being a very pleasant conventional walk across the river, the bridge is available for bridge climb adventures.

Here are some of your options:

Express Climb $119 per person, one hour.

Day Climb $129 per person, two hours.

Night Climb $139 per person, two hours.

Dawn Climb, Twilight Climb and **Climb and Abseil** $159 per person, two hours each.

Special climbs for Mandarin speakers are available and you can even get an annual pass, whatever language you speak, from $299 if you're a real enthusiast.

Address: 170 Main Street, Kangaroo Point 4169 (the southern side of the bridge)

Phone: 07 3188 9070

Website: **www.storybridgeadventureclimb.com.au**

How to get there: The most fun way to get to the bridge or the bridge climb is to walk from Central, down Creek Street to Eagle Street Pier and then catch the ferry to Kangaroo Point.

While you're in the area: Continue on to the **Riverwalk** (page 30), head across the bridge to the trendy **Howard Smith Wharves** (page 75) for something to eat.

Victoria Park Golf Course

Why you should go: While you wouldn't normally think of a golf course as a place to take the kids, Victoria Park has arguably the best mini-golf course in the country. People who've been there rave about the putt-putt course because it's just so much fun. It's also very reasonably priced for what you get. After the rigors of putt-putt you might want to have a meal at the Victoria Park Bistro, where you can get a weekday lunch of wood-fired pizza and putt-putt or a driving-range deal for just $29 per person that makes the whole experience even better value; available between 11.30 am and 3.00 pm Monday to Friday.

Address: 309 Herston Road, Herston 4006

Phone: 07 3252 0666

Website: **www.victoriapark.com.au**

How to get there: There are several options, but the easiest that requires the least amount of walking, is to walk from Central to Ann Street stop 8 and catch bus 234 to Queen Street stop 67 near Ann Street and then switch to bus 360 to Bramston Terrace at Weightman Street, stop 9, Herston. From there you walk south along Wyndham Street and Herston Road until you reach the golf course. The whole trip takes about 30 minutes. Feel free to ask the bus driver for clarification.

Opening hours: 6.00 am to 10.00 pm Sunday to Thursday, and to 11.00 pm Friday and Saturday.

Time budget: About an hour for putt putt, about an hour for pizza, about an hour for travel.

How much? Adults $20, students $17, children (under 18) $14. If you're going as a family it's a blanket deal of $14 per person.

While you're in the area: You're not all that far from **Brisbane Showgrounds** where there is usually something going on.

Feel free to visit the website, **www.brisbaneshowgrounds.com.au** or give them a call on 07 3253 3900 to see what's on. It's also the site of the **Royal Queensland Show** if you happen to be there at the right time of year (page 125). Putt putt is also available at Mermaid Beach, Gold Coast; Address: 2492 Gold Coast Highway, Mermaid Beach, 4218; Phone: 07 5575 3381; Website: **www.puttputtgolf.com.au**.

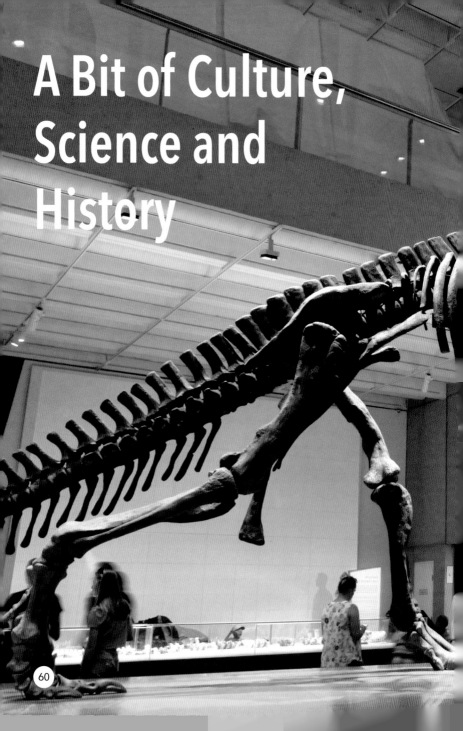

A Bit of Culture, Science and History

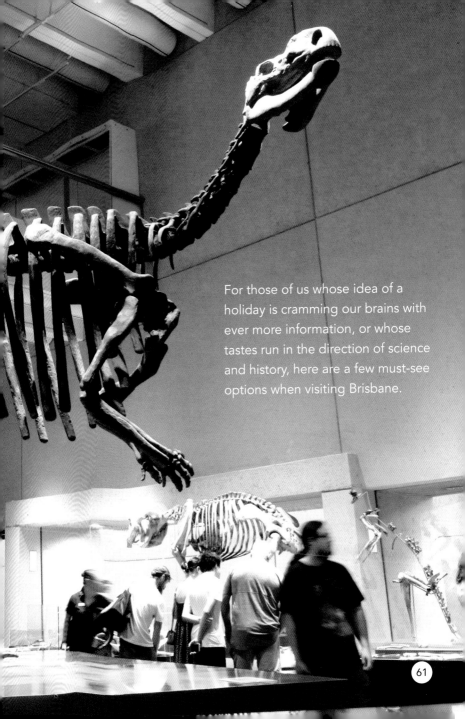

For those of us whose idea of a holiday is cramming our brains with ever more information, or whose tastes run in the direction of science and history, here are a few must-see options when visiting Brisbane.

Brisbane Jazz Club

Why you should go: Because jazz fandom is on the rise, and the Brisbane jazz scene is alive and healthy. The Jazz Club is one of the city's best-kept secrets and *the* place to go if you're into improvisation, syncopation and a cool riff or two.

In spite of its name, the Brisbane Jazz Club isn't just limited to jazz, but features an eclectic program of local, interstate and international acts. The riverside location lends itself to great views and as an extra bonus, you can eat there too!

Address: 1 Annie Street, Kangaroo Point 4169

Phone: 07 3391 2006

Website: **www.brisbanejazzclub.com.au**

How to get there: From Central, walk down Creek Street to Eagle Street Pier and then catch the ferry to Kangaroo Point. It's practically right at the ferry stop.

Opening hours: 6.30 pm to 11.00 pm Thursday and Friday, 3.00 pm to 11.00 pm Saturday, 9.30 am to 1.30 pm then 5.00 pm to 10.00 pm Sunday.

Time budget: Several hours.

How much? A typical night out costs $30 per person for non-members, $20 per person for members and budget an extra $50 per person for a three-course meal.

While you're in the area: As an extra, extra bonus, on the first Thursday of every month, you can join Jazz Singer's Jam Night, and sing along with a three-piece jazz band. To participate, contact Ingrid James (**www.ingridjames.com/jam-nights.php**).

Museum of Brisbane

Why you should go: Because this charming little museum that's tucked in **Brisbane City Hall** has items it's been gathering since 1859. Its eclectic collection includes paintings and ceramics and the focus is on Brisbane and its history. It also hosts free and paid special exhibitions all year round.

Address: City Hall, 64 Adelaide Street, Brisbane 4000

Phone: 07 3339 0800

Website: **www.museumofbrisbane.com.au**

How to get there: It's a two-minute walk south-west from Central. Just follow Ann Street for two blocks then take a right (south) along Albert Street and you're there.

Opening hours: 10.00 am to 5.00 pm every day but stays open until 7.00 pm on Fridays.

Time budget: About an hour.

How much? FREE! But like all free venues, donations are gratefully accepted.

While you're in the area: Take a FREE tour of the **Brisbane City Hall Clock Tower**. It takes 15 minutes. When you're finished, you're only a stone's throw from the delights of **Queen Street Mall** (page 39) and the **Brisbane Visitor Information and Booking Centre** (page 23).

Queensland Maritime Museum

Why you should go: Being a major coastal city with a long, winding river, Brisbane has a rich maritime history. This lovely museum is staffed by volunteers and the enthusiasm and love that they put into the museum is there in every exhibit.

The collection is not only representative of Brisbane and Queensland but includes items from all over the world. This is the sort of place you'd go to even if you weren't particularly interested in boats and ships because it will win you over.

And if you're a fan of all things nautical it's a little bit of heaven.

Address: 420 Brunswick Street, Fortitude Valley 4006

Phone: 07 3844 5361

Website: **www.maritimemuseum.com.au**

How to get there: The easy way from Central is to catch the train to South Bank Station and then it's a short walk east. The FREE **CityHopper ferry** (page 21) also has a Maritime Museum stop.

Opening hours: 9.30 am to 4.30 pm, seven days.

Time budget: At least a couple of hours, four if you really want to do it justice.

How much? Adults $16, children $7, concessions $14, families (2 adults and up to 3 children under 15) $38.

While you're in the area: You're just south of **South Bank** (page 33) and if you go a little further north, you'll be in the **Queensland Cultural Centre** (page 67). Feel free to continue a journey on the **CityHopper** (page 21) and explore the river.

If you happen to be there on a Friday evening or a weekend, consider visiting the **Collective Markets** and the **Young Designers Market** (page 119).

Institute of Modern Art and the Judith Wright Centre of Contemporary Arts

Why you should go: Ahhh, modern art! You either love it or you hate it. And if you love it then the **Institute of Modern Art** is where you can get your Brisbane dose of it. The Institute's collection features local, national and international artists with a combination of permanent collections and innovative special exhibitions throughout the year. Founded in 1975 the Institute was actually a pioneer – Australia's first dedicated space for contemporary and modern art, a fact that it's justly proud of.

Address: 420 Brunswick Street, Fortitude Valley 4006

Phone: 07 3252 5750

Website: **www.ima.org.au**

How to get there: Catch the train from Central to Fortitude Valley. Go left down Alfred Street until you reach Brunswick Street, then turn left and walk down Brunswick for a 10-minute stroll until you get to the Judith Wright Centre for Contemporary Arts.

Opening hours: 11.00 am to 6.00 pm Tuesday to Saturday and open until 9.00 pm on the first Thursday of every month.

Time budget: At least a couple of hours.

How much? FREE! Donations gratefully accepted. Extra charges for some special exhibitions.

For the virtual visitor: For the institute's 40th anniversary in 2015, the museum has a dedicated virtual gallery at **www.40years.ima.org.au**.

While you're in the area: The **Judith Wright Centre** is home to a number of performing arts organizations, so if you time it right, you might catch a performance or an event at 'The Judy'.

Phone: 07 3872 9000.

Website: **www.arts.qld.gov.au/judith-wright-centre-brisbane**.

Queensland Cultural Centre

At the northern end of Brisbane's South Bank and bounded by Kurilpa Point Park to the north, the Brisbane River to the east, Melbourne Street to the south and Grey Street to the west lies the Queensland Cultural Centre (QCC). It's home to:

- The State Library of Queensland
- The Queensland Museum and Science Centre
- Queensland Art Gallery and Gallery of Modern Art (QAGOMA), which also houses the Australian Cinémathèque and the Children's Art Centre
- Queensland Performing Arts Centre (QPAC)

It's really easy to get to. Just catch the train from Central to South Brisbane Station and you're just across the road from the Queensland Cultural Centre.

If you'd like to plan your trip beforehand, consider downloading the Culturalist app from **www.arts.qld.gov.au/culturalist**.

State Library of Queensland

Why you should go: If you're a bibliophile, if you want to know more about Brisbane, or if you just want a quiet place to relax, then you can enjoy a couple of hours of peace here. The State Library of Queensland houses a number of specialist collections, including:

- The largest collection of books in the world specifically on the subject of Queensland and its history.
- An extensive genealogical collection for those wanting to explore family history.
- An art and design collection that not only includes books but other materials related to art history dating form pre-history to the present day and an Asia Pacific design library.

The library also has:

- **The Corner**: an interactive environment for children and an indoor block playground, the Imagination Playscape.

- **The Edge**: a unique creativity space where you can create and work on all sorts of projects, with free facilities, equipment, hardware and software available.
- **kuril dhagun**: a space where Aboriginal and Torres Strait Islander people can connect with the library's services and collections.

The library also hosts exhibitions for both adults and children, especially during Queensland school holidays, and there's a cafe and shop too.

Address: Stanley Place, within the QCC.

Phone: 07 3840 7666

Website: **www.slq.qld.gov.au**

Opening hours: 10.00 am to 8.00 pm Monday to Thursday and 10.00 am to 5.00 pm Friday to Sunday.

Time budget: At least an hour.

How much? FREE!

Queensland Museum and Science Centre

Why you should go: Because it's one of those museums that combines the traditional, exhibition-oriented museum layout with fun, interactive exhibits in the tradition of Canberra's Questacon, Melbourne's Scienceworks and Sydney's Powerhouse – a safe space where your inner nerd can run free and enjoy discovering stuff. Highlights include **Wild State**, showcasing the five principle ecological environments of Queensland and their floras and faunas, and the **Lost Creatures** exhibition.

Address: Grey Street, within the QCC.

Phone: 07 3840 7555

Website: **www.qm.qld.gov.au**

Opening hours: 9.30 am to 5.00 pm, seven days.

Time budget: At least a couple of hours.

How much? FREE! But there are additional charges for some exhibitions and special events. The **SparkLab Science Centre**, within the museum, has 40 interactive exhibits and bookings are required. Adults $15, concessions $13.50, children (5–15) $12.50, families (2 adults, 2 children or 1 adult, 3 children) $46, Health Care Card holders and their children $10.

The Museum is also part of the Queensland Museum Network that includes **The Workshops Rail Museum**.

Address: North Street, North Ipswich 4305; Phone: 07 3432 5100

Website: **www.theworkshops.qm.qld.gov.au**; open 9.30 am to 4.00 pm seven days. Adults $14.50, concessions $12.50, children (3–15) $11.50, families (2 adults and up to 4 children) $44.50, children under 3 FREE! It's a 90-minute journey each way from Central, but totally worth it if you're a rail enthusiast.

Queensland Art Gallery and Gallery of Modern Art (QAGOMA)

Why you should go: Because it combines the best of both worlds of pre-modern and modern art in one venue. The range of exhibitions and collections is dazzling in its breadth and depth and there should be something here to satisfy any art lover. **Open Studio (www.qagoma.qld.gov.au/whats-on/exhibitions/open-studio)** even allows you to observe artists as they create their work.

Address: Stanley Place, within the QCC.

Phone: 07 3840 7303

Website: **www.qagoma.qld.gov.au**

Opening hours: 10.00 am to 5.00 pm, seven days.

Time budget: At least a couple of hours.

How much? FREE! But there are additional charges for some exhibitions.

While you're in the area: QAGOMA is also home to:

Australian Cinémathèque: GOMA's in-house cinema which shows both FREE and ticketed films, including unusual documentaries and rare films that you seldom get an opportunity to see the way they were originally meant to be seen, *on a big screen.* Website: **www.qagoma.qld.gov.au/whats-on/cinema**.

Children's Art Centre: A FREE discovery space to make art accessible and interactive for children, especially very young kids. Website: **www.qagoma.qld.gov.au/whats-on/kids**.

Queensland Performing Arts Centre (QPAC)

Why you should go: What cultural center would be complete without showcasing performing arts too? The first 'performance' is the building itself – striking, brutalist with a river frontage to die for. Within you'll find venues for performances of contemporary and classical music; musicals and opera; modern dance and ballet; and drama, comedy and circus.

Address: Corner of Grey Street and Melbourne Street, within the QCC.

Phone: 136 246

Website: **www.qpac.com.au**

The Creatory has a lot of articles and videos to browse through for your peak behind the scenes at QPAC: **www.qpac.com.au/the-creatory**.

While you're here: There are a number of venues to eat and drink at QPAC (**www.qpac.com.au/eat-drink**): **Bistro by QPAC**, **Cafe by QPAC**, **Lyrebird** restaurant and **Russell Street Wine Bar** as well as the theater bars.

Nice if You Have the Time

While every city has its must-sees, there are always a few little gems sprinkled here and there that are worth a visit if you have a little more time on your hands.

Howard Smith Wharves

Why you should go: Just below the northern end of the Story Bridge, the wharves date from 1935 but since it opened in late 2018 after restoration and redevelopment, Howard Smith Wharves has become a dining and events precinct. During the day it's family-friendly and accessible (although admittedly not a super-fun place for kids) and a nice place to have fish and chips or a hamburger, with greenery and parklands. At night, it's more of a grown-up playground with trendy bars, Felons Brewing Co., and a range or eateries.

Address: Under the Story Bridge, 5 Boundary Street, Brisbane City 4000

Phone: 07 3188 9090

Website: **www.howardsmithwharves.com**

How to get there: From Central take a short walk south through Anzac Square until you get to Adelaide Street. Turn right (west) until you reach the bus stop on the north side of Adelaide Street for the 199 bus. Take the bus to Adelaide Street near Boundary Street and from there it's a short walk due east. Since it's right under the northern end of Story Bridge it's hard to miss.

Opening hours: Open all the time but check for times for individual businesses.

Time budget: About half an hour for a quick look – longer if you linger for coffee or brunch, much longer if you stay for beer or a meal.

While you're in the area: Take the **Riverwalk** (page 30).

Visit the **Felons Brewing Co.** (page 158).

Old Windmill Observatory:
The Tower Mill and Surrounding Parks

Why you should go: Because the Old Windmill is charming and it's the oldest convict-built structure in Queensland, dating from the 1820s. The mill is the centerpiece of **Observatory Park** and has a long and interesting history. Right next door to the east is **King Edward Park** that's nice for a short stroll. You'll be going through it on your way to the windmill because it's just west of Central Station. Further to the west there's **Wickham Park**, somewhat larger than either King Edward or Observatory parks. If you stroll north-west and cross Albert Street, you'll be in **Roma Park**, where you'll find nice little features such as Sunset Glade, Enchanted Garden and Spectacle Garden. The **Moonlight Cinema** is also there and open in the high summer months from November; Website: **www.moonlight.com.au/brisbane/program**.

From there you can go to Roma Street Station and walk straight through it to Roma Street busway, where you can catch bus 61. Two stops and three minutes later you'll be right across the road from **Suncorp Stadium** where major sporting events and occasional rock concerts are held.

Address: Spring Hill 4000

Opening hours: The Windmill and parks are open all the time. Suncorp Stadium opening hours depend on the event.

Time budget: At least an hour.

How much? FREE! But charges apply to the Moonlight Cinema.

While you're in the area: On a very hot day you can go to the **Ithaca Swimming Pool**, just north of the stadium; Phone: 07 3369 2624; Website: **www.ithaca-pool.com.au**.

You're right near **Newstead Brewing Co** (page 158) and **XXXX Brewery** tours (page 159).

MacArthur Museum

Why you should go: If you're interested in the part Australia played in World War II, the MacArthur Museum building was the headquarters for much of the South West Pacific Area operations and the museum focuses on Brisbane during the war years and the alliance between Australia and the United States. You can even sit at the desk of General Douglas MacArthur, Commander in Chief of the Allied Forces in the South West Pacific Area.

Address: Level 8 MacArthur Chambers, 201 Edward Street, Brisbane 4000

Phone: 07 3211 7052

Website: **www.mmb.org.au**

How to get there: From Central walk south-west down Ann Street until you get to Edward Street and turn left, then walk down Edward Street to the corner of Queen Street.

Opening hours: 10.00 am to 3.00 pm Tuesday, Thursday and Sunday.

Time budget: At least an hour.

How much? Adults $10, everyone else $5, families $20.

While you're in the area: You're in the heart of the city and everything it has to offer but particularly close to the **Queen Street shopping precinct** (page 39).

The Gabba

Why you should go: In the winter months, it's the AFL. In the summer months, it's cricket, including the Sheffield Shield (since 1931), and it all happens at the Brisbane Cricket Ground. But nobody calls it that. To practically everyone it's The Gabba – named after the suburb Woolloongabba, which possibly meant 'fight talk place', appropriate for a ground of competition and contest. It seats around 36,000 and also holds soccer, rugby league and rugby union matches, the occasional concert and special event. For many attending an event at The Gabba is a quintessentially Brisbane experience.

Address: Vulture Street, Woolloongabba 4102

Phone: 1300 843 422

Website: **www.thegabba.com.au**

How to get there: From Central walk to Ann Street stop 8. Catch bus 212 to Woolloongabba Bus Station. From there it's a short walk east. During the cricket and AFL seasons public transport is included FREE with your event ticket.

How much? A weekly behind-the-scenes tour runs on Thursdays at 11.00 am. Bookings essential. Adults $16, children (4–17) $6, children under 4 FREE! General admission to an AFL game or to a cricket match can cost as little as $10 per ticket, plus a handling fee per transaction. Admission to the Sheffield Shield matches is FREE! If you love cricket, and you're there at the time, why wouldn't you?

While you're in the area: **South Bank** (page 33) and the **Queensland Cultural Centre** (page 67) are just a short bus ride west.

The Great Outdoors

Thanks to the climate of south-east Queensland Brisbane is an outdoorsy city. Even better, Brisbane is close to a number of fine destinations that bring you even closer to nature so that visitors and locals alike have easy access to outdoor fun, all within a few hours of the CBD and ideal for day trips or weekends.

Australia Zoo

Why you should go: Established by Bob and Lyn Irwin in 1970, Australia Zoo will always be associated with their larger-than-life son, Steve, and the late Crocodile Hunter's legacy lives on in this 400-hectare (1000-acre) zoo and wildlife sanctuary, still owned by his widow, Terri Irwin. Highlights include the **Mount Franklin Crocoseum**, a 5000-seat stadium for bird, crocodile and snake shows; the **Africa Safari Exhibit**; **Bindi's Island**, with its panoramic view of the zoo; **Rainforest Aviary**, **South-East Asian Precinct**, the **Tiger Temple** and two shaded playgrounds. You can even do whale watching at Mooloolaba on *Whale One*. It's a completely immersive experience.

Address: 1638 Steve Irwin Way, Beerwah 4519

Phone: 07 5436 2000

Website: **www.australiazoo.com.au**

How to get there: From Central catch the train to Beerwah Station. Travel time is about 75 minutes then wait for the zoo's FREE shuttle bus. It'll be at bus stop 649. It's white and has a snake on it. You can also get the shuttle bus back at the end of your visit.

Opening hours: 9.00 am to 5.00 pm seven days.

Time budget: It's at least a whole day trip.

How much? Prices depend on whether you want a one-day or two-day pass. Yearly passes are also available. At the very least you're looking at about $59 for adults, pensioners and students $47, children $35, and families (2 adults, 2 children) $172.

While you're in the area: Seriously consider the two-day pass. Australia Zoo can provide recommendations on where to stay in the area. You can also use your stay as a base for visiting the **Sunshine Coast** (page 104), the **Big Pineapple** and **Wildlife HQ** (page 86).

The Big Pineapple, Treetop Challenge and the Wildlife HQ Zoo

Why you should go: Because it's big and it's an iconic and fun celebration of all things pineapply. There's the heritage-listed Big Pineapple Train with a steep and curving track through

the surrounding rainforest and orchids and the new Treetop Challenge for the more adventurous. The Wildlife HQ is a great small zoo for those who don't want or need the commitment of visiting **Australia Zoo** (page 84).

Address: 76 Nambour Connection Road, Woombye 4559

Phone: 1800 132 289

Website: **www.bigpineapple.com.au**

How to get there: From Central it's a train trip to Woombye then a walk to Wakefield Street to catch bus 636 to Nambour. It's a two-hour journey. But you're better off visiting as part of a trip to the **Sunshine Coast** (page 104), where you're only looking at a 20-minute bus ride on route 610 from Maroochydore Station to Nambour.

Opening hours: 8.30 am to 4.00 pm seven days.

Time budget: At least a couple of hours if you're planning to do the Treetop Challenge or visit the zoo.

How much? FREE to visit the Big Pineapple. The Pineapple Train is $5 per person.

While you're in the area: **The Treetop Challenge** comprises up to 100 challenges in an adventure park, which involve climbing, flying foxes and ziplines and being in various states of suspension in the canopy of a tropical rainforest.

Phone: 07 5306 1033; Website: **www.treetopchallenge.com.au/ sunshine-coast-adventure**; adults $55, concessions $50, children (8–14) $45. Bookings essential.

The **Wildlife HQ Zoo** is home to over 200 animal species from around the world with a large primate collection.

Phone: 0428 660 671; Website: **www.whqzoo.com**; open 9.00 am to 4.00 pm seven days. Adults $29, seniors $22, children (3–15) $15, under 3s FREE!

Moreton Island and Tangalooma

Why you should go: 58 kilometers (36 miles) north-east of Brisbane over Moreton Bay lies Moreton Island, the traditional home of the Ngugi people. Some 98 per cent of its 186 square kilometers (72 square miles) is a national park where, in many parts, you can camp and galivant around in a four-wheel drive, which is recommended as the island has no sealed roads. It's a popular destination for day trips or short-stay trips because there's lots to see and do, including bird and whale watching, snorkeling (especially around the Tangalooma wrecks), diving and fishing, parasailing and sand tobogganing. Tangalooma ('where the fish gather'), a resort on the island's west coast, was originally a whaling station and is now the place to go when you want the fun of feeding dolphins.

Website: **www.visitmoretonisland.com**; **www.tangalooma.com**

How to get there: You'll need to get to the ferry terminal early, at about 7.00 am. Moreton Island Adventures (Phone: 07 3909 3333; Website: **www.moretonislandadventures.com.au**) runs a ferry service called the Micat from the terminal at 14 Howard Smith Drive, Port of Brisbane 4178. Catch a train to Wynnum Station (40 minutes). From there, it's a 10-minute taxi ride to the terminal. Tangalooma Resort operates its own transfers from its terminal at 220 Holt Street, Pinkenba 4009. From Central take the train to Toombul Station. Walk east to Toombul Shopping Centre and take bus 590 to Kingsford Smith Drive at Holt Street. From there, catch a cab. The whole trip takes about 45 minutes.

The catamaran from Brisbane take a further 75 minutes to get to the island. For further information, go to: **www.getyourguide.com** and enter 'Moreton Island' in the Search.

How much? A Ferry and Adventure day pass starts from as little as $99 per person. A Moreton Island day trip with three-hour whale watching cruise starts at about $129 per person. A Moreton Island dolphin and snorkel cruise adventure starts at about $149.

North Stradbroke Island

Why you should go: North and South Stradbroke Islands were just 'Stradbroke Island' until a storm in 1896 separated the two, but at just over 275 square kilometers (106 square miles) North Stradbroke is still the world's second largest sand island, after Fraser Island, not that far to the north and over six times bigger. The traditional home of the Quandamooka people is now home to over 2000 non-Indigenous people who mainly live in the townships of Dunwich, Point Lookout and Amity Point.

Visitors to the island can enjoy the abundant wildlife both on land and in the sea. Like **Moreton Island** to the north (page 88) there's plenty of the sorts of things that people do on islands but the feel of North Stradbroke is a little more sedate, a little less developed. Highlights of the island include its many lakes (particularly Blue Lake), springs (particularly Myora Springs) and wetlands (particularly Eighteen Mile Swamp – the largest of its kind in the world) and rare plants and animals you won't find anywhere else.

Website: **www.stradbrokeisland.com**

How to get there: First, get to Cleveland station from Central by train. This takes about an hour. From there, Stradbroke Flyer Water Taxis will provide you with a free shuttle bus to the wharf. From there the Flyer takes about 25 minutes. Return fares cost: adults $20, students $15, pensioners and children $10, families $50; Phone: 07 3821 3821; Website: **www.flyer.com.au**. Alternatively, especially if you have a vehicle, **Stradbroke Ferries** start at $97 return: Phone: 1300 787 232. Website: **www.stradbrokeferries.com.au**.

How much? You can walk around and spend nothing or spend as much as you like on the various offerings to amuse and delight you.

While you're in the area: Once a year there's **Island Vibe**, North Stradbroke's music and arts festival held in late October; (Website: **www.islandvibe.com.au**).

Why take a car or walk when you can hire a scooter that you can drive with either a car licence or a P plate? Phone: 0497 777 933. Website: **www.scootersonstraddie.com.au**.

Learn to surf at the **North Stradbroke Surf School** from $50, Phone: 0407 642 616.

Bribie Island and Sandstone Point

Why you should go: The smallest of the Moreton Bay sand islands, Bribie is only 148 square kilometers (57 square miles). One third of it is national park, and much of the rest of it is conifer plantations closed to public access. It's so close to the coast that you can get to it by a road bridge from Sandstone Point. Both the point and island are basically outer, outer suburbs of Brisbane (or the **Sunshine Coast** (page 104), depending on your point of view) and their big advantage is that the area is very accessible, very reasonably priced and very family friendly.

Address: Bribie Island Visitor Information Centre, Benabrow Avenue, Bellara 4507

Phone: 07 3408 9026

Website: **www.visitbribieisland.com.au**

How to get there: Train from Central to Caboolture Station (50 minutes), then Translink runs a bus service around Bribie Island and to Sandstone Point and Caboolture. Check the website for details: **www.translink.com.au**.

Time budget: Easily a whole day trip.

How much? Depends on where you go and what you do.

While you're in the area: Please note that no domestic animals are allowed within the national park area and if a ranger catches you with one, even if it hasn't left your vehicle, you're in for a fine.

Visit the **Bribie Island Seaside Museum:** 1 South Esplanade, Bongaree, 4507

Phone: 07 3408 0007; Website: **www.moretonbay.qld.gov.au/ Galleries-Museums/Locations/Seaside-Museum**

Open: 10.00 am to 4.00 pm Tuesday to Friday, 10.00 am to 3.00 pm Saturday and Sunday; entry FREE!

Bribie Island Butterfly House is a great place to take the kids for an hour or two: 208 First Avenue, Bongaree 4507

Phone: 0459 104 174; Website: **www.bribieislandbutterflyhouse.org**; open on Sunday and Wednesday from 10.00 am to 4.00 pm.

Take a colorful hat, it attracts the butterflies!

At **Sandstone Point** you can hire a jet ski, or a four-wheel drive or a boat.

The Gold Coast and Its Theme Parks

A mere 66 kilometers (40 miles) south of Brisbane and just north of the border with New South Wales, Gold Coast has almost 600,000 permanent inhabitants, making it the most populous non-capital city in Australia. But around 10 million tourists visit it every year, which means Gold Coast lives, breathes, eats and drinks tourism. It is a city virtually devoted to being a place to have fun in.

Why is it so popular? Is it the 60 kilometers (37 miles) of golden-sanded beaches? Is it the 600 kilometers (370 miles) of canals? Is it the weather that is generally warm and sunny all year round? Is it the golden bikini-clad meter maids? The surf carnivals? The Gold Coast 600 car race? So many questions! In any case, arguably the highlight of the Gold Coast is the entertainment worlds.

If you want to find out what's on at the Gold Coast go to **www.destinationgoldcoast.com** or visit **Destination Gold Coast**, 2 Cavil Lane, Surfers Paradise 4217; Phone: 1300 309 440; open 8.30 am to 5.00 pm Monday to Friday, 9.00 am to 6.00 pm Saturday and 9.00 am to 4.00 pm Sunday.

Getting there: Easy, as trains to the Gold Coast regularly leave Brisbane and take about an hour. Bus route TX7 links Coomera, **Dreamworld**, Helensvale, **Movie World** and the theme parks and attractions near it. **Movie World**, **Paradise Country**, **Wet 'n' Wild**, **Top Golf** and **Australian Outback Spectacular** are all within walking distance of each other.

Time budget: Up to you, but realistically each theme park is an all-day commitment, especially if you're traveling from Brisbane. If you were to visit all of them it would take at the very least *four very full days*, longer if you wanted a more leisurely approach.

Dreamworld and WhiteWater World

Why you should go: Australia's biggest theme park is just one, big, crazy, permanent carnival covering 85 hectares (210 acres) making it twice the size of Vatican City and a lot more upbeat. Its 27 attractions are organized by themed area – Dreamworld Corroboree, Dreamworks Experience, Riverworld, Rocky Hollow, Tiger Island, Ocean Parade, Town of Gold Rush as well as ABC World and Wiggles World, where the toddlers will be most at home. Main Street is where you'll find food, drink and merchandise. Also located on the grounds is Dreamworld Studios, where *Big Brother* Australia was filmed. WhiteWater World a water park, is just next door and your Dreamworld pass allows you access there too. There are also shows and events and animal experiences too.

Address: Dreamworld Parkway, Coomera 4209
Phone: 07 5588 1111
Website: **www.dreamworld.com.au**

How to get there: Take the train from Central to Coomera Station then go to bus stop B, take the TX7 bus to Dreamworld. Station to gate is a 10-minute journey.

Opening hours: 10.00 am to 5.00 pm, seven days. Summer school holiday extension hours to 7.00 pm.

How much? You can get one, three and seven-day passes starting from adults $95, everybody else $85 and families $320 (2 adults, 2 children 3–13), children under 3 FREE! Annual passes aren't much more: adults $129, everybody else $99 and families $360 (2 adults, 2 children 3–13).

While you're in the area: Please note that for safety reasons some rides have height restrictions. Also, because the park is open every day the only time to do maintenance is during opening hours, which means that from time to time some rides are closed.

Check the website for information on both these restrictions. Animal experiences are separately booked and paid for.

Warner Bros. Movie World and Paradise Country

Why you should go: This theme park is especially linked to Hollywood popcorn blockbusters, especially the DC Comics movie franchises, and park rides change every few years depending on what's currently 'in'. You can even be a Hollywood stunt driver or get an Access All Areas Star Tour (**www.themeparks.com.au/attractions/warner-bros-movie-world**).

Paradise Country is just down the road and focuses on farm animals and farm life, wild animals and cuddly experiences that are perfect for younger children and is about as close as you'll get to experiencing a Queensland farm without actually visiting a Queensland farm. You can even do a farmstay there.

Address: Entertainment Road/Pacific Motorway, Oxenford 4210

Phone: 133 386

Website: **www.movieworld.com.au**; **www.paradisecountry.com.au**

How to get there: Central to Helensvale Station then from stop C take bus TX7 to Movie World.

Opening hours: Movie World: 9.30 am to 5.00 pm, seven days; Paradise Country: 9.30 am to 4.30 pm.

How much? Single day passes start from $89, and three-day passes start from $129. But if you're really going to go to town on the whole theme park experience Warner Bros./Village Roadshow offer a number of really good deals. Locals can get a 12-month unlimited entry to Movie World, Sea World, Wet 'n' Wild and Paradise Country for only $149 per person. Non-locals get the same deal for $215 per person. For further details on these deals and other passes go to **www.movieworld.com.au/tickets**.

While you're in the area: At Movie World there are a number of special events that happen throughout the year. For example,

around Halloween there's Fright Night. If you happen to be at Movie World in the latter half of December you can attend the White Christmas event at night. Check the website for details.

Wet 'n' Wild, Top Golf and Australian Outback Spectacular

Why you should go: Because south-east Queensland's climate is so clement, if you like water, you could have a lot of fun at **Wet 'n' Wild**. Over one million visitors a year seem to think so too. The pools and slides are heated during the winter months making all this wetness even more attractive.

Address: Entertainment Road/Pacific Motorway, Oxenford 4210
Phone: 133 386
Website: **www.wetnwild.com.au**

Opening hours: 10.00 am to 4.00 pm in the colder months, extended to 5.00 pm from September to May.

How much? Single day entry starts at $69 per person, but for special deals see the entry for **Movie World** (page 99). During peak times **Fast Track** ($60 per person) will get you to the top of the Wet 'n' Wild queues for Aqualoop, Black Hole, Kamikaze and Tornado. Optional extras include FlowRider and SkyCoaster.

While you're in the area: **Top Golf** is a way of enjoying golfing without committing to an expensive membership at a golf club, although you can do that at Top Golf too. Prices start from $5 per person for basic lifetime membership and then from $50 per bay per hour for up to six players. For details go to **www.topgolf.com.au**. Phone: 1300 008 442; open 9.00 am to 10.00 pm Sunday to Thursday and until midnight on Friday and Saturday.

Australian Outback Spectacular is an immersive experience that's a bit like a high-tech, three-course-dinner theater show that gives you a taste of the entire continent in just a few hours. Shows commence from around 6.30 pm each evening with a Sunday matinee from about midday. Prices start at adults $99, children $69; Phone: 133 386; Website: **www.outbackspectacular.com.au**.

Sea World

Why you should go: Sea World is located just across the way from Main Beach on a peninsula that juts out of the Gold Coast suburb of Southport. It's a spectacular location that the theme park takes full advantage of. What do you get for your entry? Marine animal shows, including penguins, seals, Australia's

only polar bear exhibit and the world's largest human-made lagoon for sharks. There are also rides, interactive tours and an oceanarium. They even successfully breed dolphins there at the dolphin nursery! You can also stay at **Sea World Resort**, which is just next door and there are a variety of package deals available: **www.seaworld.com.au/resort/package-deals**.

Address: Sea World Drive, Main Beach 4217

Phone: 133 386

Website: **www.seaworld.com.au**

How to get there: Take the train from Central to Helensvale Station then at bus stop D catch bus 704 to Sea World. Total trip time from Central to Sea World is almost two hours, so you'd better start early.

Opening hours: 9.30 am to 5.00 pm, seven days.

How much? Single day entry starts at $79 per person, but for special multi-venue, multi-entry deals see the entry for **Movie World** (page 99) and see below for Sea World Resort deals.

While you're in the area: Extras include a variety of animal adventures which include swimming and feeding the sea life. **Sea World Cruises** can take you on trips through the Gold Coast canals and during the winter months when whales are migrating you can do a Sea World whale watch. They last 2½ hours and happen 4 times a day. Whale watching can be part of a Sea World Resort package deal starting from $279 per room, twin share. Phone: 1300 139 677 if you have trouble interpreting the website – we did! Website: **www.seaworld.com.au/resort**.

Carnivale happens for a week once a year in January and features light shows, live music, food and family entertainment: **www.seaworldcarnivale.com.au/event-info/event-dates**.

Tamborine Mountain

OK, so it's a little out of the way and off the beaten tourist track but if you really want to go somewhere different try Tamborine Mountain/ Mount Tamborine.

Located a good 55 kilometers (35 miles) south of Brisbane as the crow flies there's no public transport there, but there are still a few options if you don't have your own car.

- Edison Miraziz is a small operator who's happy to take a group of up to six to Mount Tamborine for around $120 each way for the whole group. He'll never charge you more than an Uber would. 24-hours' notice preferred. Phone: 0407 779 991 to discuss your plans.
- Queensland Day Tours; Phone: 0488 332 257.
- Southern Cross Tours; Phone: 1300 762 665.
- Tours on Tamborine; Phone: 0438 174 631;
  Website: **www.toursontamborine.com.au**.

Highlights of Tamborine Mountain include:
Glow worm caves: human-made caves with luminescent worms.

Cedar Creek Estate, 104–144 Harley Road, Tamborine Mountain 4272; Phone: 07 5545 1666; Website: **www.glowwormcavetamborinemountain.com.au**; open 10.00 am to 4.00 pm seven days with extended hours on Friday and Saturday until 6.00 pm; adults $14, seniors/concessions $10.80, children (4–12) $6, under 4s FREE!

Hot air ballooning with Hot Air Ballooning Scenic Rim; Phone: 07 4039 9942; Website: www.hotair.com.au.

Tamborine Rainforest Skywalk: Adventure park featuring zip-lining and treetop courses that include climbs, bridge walks and drops; Cedar Creek Falls Road and Tamborine Mountain Road, Tamborine Mountain 4272; Phone: 07 5661 9038; Website: **www.treetopchallenge.com.au**; open 10.00 am to 5.00 pm Monday to Friday but opens at 8.30 am on weekends; prices from adults $55, children $45 and family (2 adults, 2 children) $180.

There are also a lot of **wineries**, **distilleries, restaurants** and **galleries** in the area.

Feel free to explore **www.visittamborinemountain.com.au**.

The Sunshine Coast

After Brisbane and the Gold Coast the Sunshine Coast is the most populated part of Queensland. Over 300,000 people live in this coast-hugging area, 100 kilometers (62 miles) north of the capital. Its centers include Caloundra, Maroochydore and Noosa Heads on the seafront and Landsborough and Nambour further inland. It's quieter and more sedate than the Gold Coast, but still sees more than three million visitors a year, many of whom take full advantage of the many beaches.

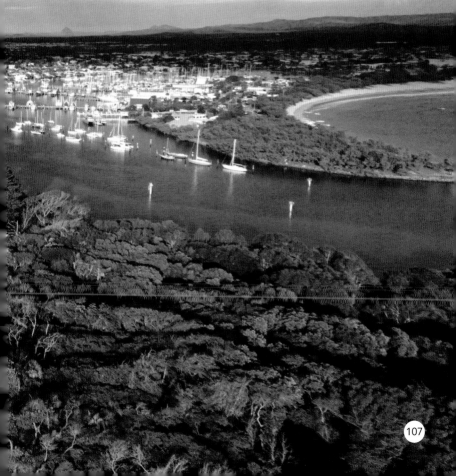

Getting there is relatively easy. For example, a train from Central to Landsborough will take about 80 to 90 minutes. From there you can catch bus 615 to Maroochydore – a further 45 minutes. If you stay on the bus it will magically transform into route 620 and take you on to Noosa Heads if you so choose. This will take a further hour. It might seem like a long trip, but it's very pretty and totally worth it if you have the time.

Your go-to place for further information about the delights of the Sunshine Coast is **www.visitsunshinecoast.com**. Here you'll find suggestions for the various regions, including: Caloundra, Coolum, Eumundi, Hinterland, Kawana, Maroochydore, Mooloolaba, Nambour, Noosa, Gympie and Rainbow Beach.

The site has extensive information on accommodation; adventure sports; arts, culture and heritage; attractions; beaches, nature and wildlife; markets and shopping; events; food and drink; and spas, yoga and well-being.

You can also call the **Visitor Information Centre** on 1300 847 481.

Regional attractions include **Australia Zoo** (page 84), **The Big Pineapple, Treetop Challenge and the Wildlife HQ Zoo** (page 86). Also worthy of note are:

Aussie World a theme park with over 30 rides and including a charmingly eccentric version of the Ettamogah ('place of good drink', apparently) Pub. It's a 30-minute trip on the 615 bus from

Maroochydore. Address: Downunder Drive, 73 Frizzo Road, Bruce Highway, Palmview, 4553; Phone: 07 5494 5444; Website: **www.aussieworld.com.au**; open 10.00 am to 3.00 pm Monday to Friday and until 5.00 pm on weekends; single entry $38, family (2 adults, 2 children or 1 adult, 3 children) $136, family (2 adults, 3 children or 1 adult, 4 children) $167. You can easily spend the day here.

The Buderim Ginger Factory is to all things ginger what the Big Pineapple is to all things pineapple. From Nambour, it's a 12-minute trip on the 631 bus to Yandina Station, then a 20-minute walk north. Address: 50 Pioneer Road, Yandina 4561; Phone: 1800 067 686; Website: **www.gingerfactory.com.au**; open 9.00 am to 5.00 pm seven days; Entry is FREE but there are lots of paid rides and activities too including factory tours, train and boat rides and even a bee show – it's amazing how much you can squeeze out of the ginger theme!

Also worthy of note are the **National Parks**, including Fraser Island, Glass House Mountains, Great Sandy, Kondalilla, Mapleton Falls and Noosa National Parks. Visit **www.parks.des.qld.gov.au/parks** for more details.

And if you're a real foody, you might also consider the **Curated Plate** festival (page 145).

SEA LIFE Sunshine Coast Aquarium

Why you should go: Because it showcases sea life through three
habitats – cave, coral reef and open ocean.

Highlights include seal shows, jellyfish tours, a touch pool and
behind-the-scenes tours.

Address: Parkyn Parade, Mooloolaba 4557

Phone: 07 5458 6226

Website: **www.underwaterworld.com.au**

How to get there: From Maroochydore bus station platform 1
take the 600 bus to River Esplanade. From there, it's a short walk
east. Total time about 15 minutes.

Opening hours: 9.00 am to 3.00 pm seven days.

Time budget: At least a couple of hours.

How much? General admission from adults $32 and children $22
but see the next page for a deal.

The Merlin Pass

SEA LIFE Gold Coast is part of the Merlin Group of Attractions. The **Merlin Annual Pass** allows you to see 10 attractions in Australia and New Zealand and represents excellent value for money, especially if you plan to visit Sydney and/or Melbourne as well as Brisbane sometime in the 12 months after purchasing the pass.

For details go to: **www.merlinannualpass.com.au**.

The pass allows unlimited visits to the following attractions:
- Kelly Tarlton's SEA LIFE Aquarium, Auckland
- Illawarra Fly Treetop Adventures
- Otway Fly Treetop Adventures
- LEGOLAND Discovery Centre, Melbourne
- SEA LIFE Melbourne Aquarium
- Madame Tussauds Sydney
- SEA LIFE Sydney Aquarium
- Sydney Tower Eye
- WILD LIFE Sydney Zoo
- and, of course, SEA LIFE Sunshine Coast

Prices start at $109 per person (individual) or $79 per person for a family (one or two adults with at least one child). From time to time the Merlin Annual Pass goes on sale so it's even better value for money.

Annual Pass holders will need to pre-book their times for some venues during weekends, school and public holidays.

Problems buying tickets online?

Call 1800 751 060 or email **supportaus@accesso.com**.

To Market, to Market!

Brisbane just *loves* its markets and whether you want food (fresh produce, artisanal or takeaway), clothing, shoes, arts, crafts or any number of the gazillion things that you can find in a market or bazaar, Brisbane has the market for you. Seriously, you'll be spoiled for choice. There's a market for every day of the week and after doing a lot of the more touristy stuff there really are few better ways of meeting the locals and getting to know the *real* Brisbane.

Brisbane MarketPlace and the Brisbane Night Market

Type: Mixed market with themed days.

Address: 250 Sherwood Road, Rocklea 4106

Phone: 07 3915 4277

Website: **www.brisbanemarketplace.com.au**

How to get there: Take the train from Central to Rocklea Station (25 minutes) then from the corner of Lillian Avenue and Olivia Avenue take bus 599 Sherwood Road at Rocklea. From there, it's a short walk south. Total trip time 45 minutes.

Opening hours: 8.00 am to 3.30 pm Monday to Thursday, 8.00 am to 2.00 pm Friday, 6.00 am to midday weekends. On Fridays there is also the **Night Market** from 4.00 pm to 10.00 pm with entertainment as well as food (**www.brisbanemarketplace.com.au/ markets/brisbane-night-market**). Saturday is the **Fresh Market**.

Sunday is the **Discovery Market** with bargain hunters rummaging through trash and treasure.

Brisbane City Markets and Reddacliff Place

Type: Farmers, growers and artisans' market with live entertainment.

Address: Reddacliff Place, Queen Street, Brisbane 4000

Phone: 0422 669 828

Website: **www.brisbanecitymarkets.com.au**

How to get there: From Central walk west along Ann Street, then turn left (south) down George Street.

Opening hours: 8.00 am to 6.00 pm Wednesday. This market also happens at Cathedral Square, 410 Ann Street, on the corner of Wharf Street, every Thursday from 8.30 am to 2.30 pm. It's a short walk north-east of Central.

Jan Powers Farmers Market, Manly Harbour Markets and Mitchelton Farmers Markets

Type: Saturday farmers' market providing local fruits and veggies, flowers, bread, meat, honey and the like.

Address: The Brisbane Powerhouse, 119 Lamington Street, New Farm 4005

Website: **www.janpowersfarmersmarkets.com.au**

How to get there: From Central catch bus 199 from stop 26 in Adelaide Street to Merthyr Road and then walk south-east (travel time about 30 minutes), or catch bus 196 from stop 25 on Adelaide Street to Brunswick Street at Parkview, or catch the FREE **CityHopper ferry** (page 21).

Opening hours: 6.00 am to midday Saturday.

This market also happens at Manly Harbour from 6.00 am to midday every second Saturday and there's also the **Manly Creative Markets** 8.00 am to 3.00 pm every second Sunday. Just take the train from Central to Manly Station then walk east along Yamboyna Street then north-east up Carlton Terrace until you hit the coast. Total travel time 50 minutes. Website: **www.manlyharbourvillage.com**.

There's also **Mitchelton Farmers Markets** on the first Sunday of each month from 6.00 am to midday. Just catch the train from Central to Mitchelton and in 20 minutes you're there.

Milton Markets, Rosalie Gourmet Market, The Bardon Markets and The Bardon Shed

There are a whole bunch of markets in walking distance of each other from Milton Station. From Central to Milton Station takes about six minutes. Ideally, you can visit all these places on a Sunday, as part of a long, leisurely, foody-oriented stroll.

Milton Markets

A five-minute walk east of the station with more than 140 stalls of fresh farm produce, live music and gifts, from 7.00 am to 1.00 pm Sunday.

Address: Milton Green, 47 Cribb Street 4064

Website: **www.miltonmarkets.com.au**.

Rosalie Gourmet Markets

More a high-end food hall than a traditional market but if you want premium and rare delicatessen goods here's where you go. It's a 10-minute walk north up Baroona Road, not far from Gregory Park. – Open 7.00 am to 7.00 pm Monday to Friday and closes at 6.00 pm weekends.

Address: 164 Baroona Road, Paddington, 4064

Phone: 07 3876 62222; Website: **www.rosaliegourmet.com.au**.

The Bardon Markets

A further 10-minute walk up Baroona Road, heading west from Rosalie Gourmet, and in Norman Buchan Park (just opposite the grounds of Queensland Government House, where you can go for a lovely stroll any day of the week). Held from 7.00 am to midday on Sundays. Website: **www.facebook.com/bardoncommunitymarkets**.

The Bardon Shed

If you then walk south through Norman Buchan Park you'll find The Bardon Shed, a large fresh food market at 8 Runic Street, Bardon 4065. Phone: 07 3369 9681; Website: **www.thebardonshed.com.au**; open 6.00 am to 7.00 pm, seven days. From there you can take the 475 bus from Boundary Road near Brown Street stop 15 to Milton Station and from there catch the train back to Central.

Riverside Markets and the CityCycle Scheme

Type: Farmer's market mixed with art, fashion and gifts where you can do coffee and brunch in the City Botanic Gardens.

Address: At the north end of City Botanic Gardens where Albert Street and Alice Street meet.

Phone: 07 3870 2807; 0415 380 771

Website: **www.theriversidemarkets.com.au**

How to get there: From Central walk south-west along Ann Street until you hit Albert Street, turn left (south) and stroll to the end (15 minutes). Or, if you happen to be near a ferry jetty remember that there's a jetty at QUT Gardens Point and you can walk through the grounds of the Queensland University of Technology then cross the City Botanic Gardens going north and that will get you there too.

Opening hours: 8.00 am to 3.00 pm every Sunday.

One really nice way of experiencing the Riverside Markets and the Botanic Gardens is to take advantage of the Brisbane CityCycle scheme. **CityCycle** bike hire is available 24 hours, 7 days a week. Located in close proximity to each other, every CityCycle station has a minimum of 10 bike racks making it an easy, reliable and convenient transport option.

To use the scheme go to **www.citycycle.com.au**. First pay your monthly access fee of $5 per month or a 24-hour access pass for $2. Once a CityCycle membership or casual pass is purchased, you can hire and return a bike at any CityCycle station within the network. Or, you can ride all day for free, as long as the bikes are returned within half-hour intervals. After this half-hour of free use expires, a usage fee applies – 31 to 60 minutes costs $2 and every 30 minutes after that is $5. The system is designed to encourage you to change your bike over frequently at different stations so that you're not hogging a single bike all day.

To find a bike station go to: **www.citycycle.com.au/All-Stations/Station-Map#**. Happy riding!

The Collective Markets and the Young Designers Market

Type: Arts, crafts, jewelry, home decor and clothing.
Address: 29 Stanley Street Plaza, South Brisbane 4101
Phone: 07 3844 2440
Website: **www.collectivemarkets.com.au**
How to get there: From Central go to South Bank Station. Walk north along Grey Street until you reach Stanley Street then turn right (east) and you're practically there.
Opening hours: 5.00 pm to 9.00 pm Friday, 10.00 am to 9.00 pm Saturday, 9.00 am to 4.00 pm Sunday.

The Young Designers Market is just what it says it is – a showcase and retail opportunity for emerging clothing designers to strut their stuff and test their wares. This market is just down the road west of the Collective Markets. It's on the corner of Stanley Street and Little Stanley Street and is open 10.00 am to 4.00 pm on the first Sunday of the month. Website: **www.youngdesignersmarket.com.au**.

The Davies Park Market and The Boundary Street Night Markets

The Davies Park Market

From 6.00 am to 2.00 pm on Saturdays in Davies Park at the corner of Montague Road and Jane Street, West End 4101; Phone: 0431 019 454; Website: **www.daviesparkmarket.com.au**. To get there take the route 60 bus from Adelaide Street stop 36 and get off at Montague Road stop 7.

Boundary Street Market

Happens from 4.00 pm to 10.00 pm on Fridays and Saturdays and on Sundays the market can be at 9.00 am to 3.00 pm or midday to 8.00 pm – check the website before visiting. Address: 55 Russell Street, West End 4101; Phone: 0409 767 497
Website: **www.boundarystreetmarkets.com.au**.

To get there, from Central take the train to South Brisbane station. Walk south-west along Melbourne Street until you reach Boundary Street, then turn left (south) into Boundary Street and you're a block away.

On Saturdays you can walk from Davies to Boundary by walking west to east along Jane Street.

Once a Year if You Can Make It

Brisbane has a number of well-known events that only happen once a year (listed here in calendar order) and you can plan your visit around them. Many of the event websites offer you the opportunity to go on an email list so that they can notify you as soon as dates and specific events are finalized.

January to December – Valley Fiesta

It's a year-long event. Does this therefore count as a 'once-a-year event'? Valley Fiesta is how Fortitude Valley likes to divide its year up into themes, sprinkled here and there with special events.
Website: **www.myvalley.com.au/valley-fiesta**

February/March – Brisbane Comedy Festival

It's not that Brisbane is an unfunny city, but it's even funnier in the late summer. You can expect dozens of acts to tickle your laughing bones for about a month, mostly at **Brisbane Powerhouse** (page 54) but also at **Brisbane City Hall**, at **Sunnybank Performing Arts & Cultural Centre (SunPAC)** in Sunnybank, and at **Newstead Brewing Company** in Milton (page 158).
Website: **www.brisbanecomedyfestival.com**

March – Big Gay Day

Brisbane's answer to Sydney's Mardi Gras is held in and around the Wickham Hotel in Fortitude Valley and is a combination of festival and fundraising event that has been welcoming 'rainbow party people' since 2001.
Website: **www.biggayday.com.au**

May Labour Day Weekend – Caxton Street Seafood and Wine Festival

A celebration of Australian music, seafood and wine that has been running for 20 years in the Caxton Street precinct, known for its nightlife and dining options.

Website: **www.caxtonstreet.com.au**

Late May – The Paniyiri Greek Festival

Around 50,000 Greeks and Hellenophiles gather at Musgrave Park and the Greek Club in Edmondstone Street in South Brisbane on the third weekend of May every year for Australia's longest running Greek festival. Eat. Stomp grapes. Eat. Dance. Eat some more …

Website: **www.brisbane-australia.com/paniyiri-greek-festival.html**

Late May/Early June – International Jazz Festival

Brisbane International Jazz Festival is a celebration of the genre with local, interstate and international acts at a variety of venues throughout the city.

Website: **www.bijf.com.au**

June to August – Brisbane Marathon Festival

Attracting visitors from over two dozen countries the marathon is something to build your visit around if running long distances is your idea of a good time.

Website: **www.brisbanemarathon.com**

July – South Bank's Regional Flavours Food and Wine Festival

Regional Flavours is Australia's largest free food and wine festival and is held in Brisbane's picturesque South Bank Parklands. Enjoy free entertainment from celebrity chefs and cooks, live music, street food stalls, kids' activities and a thriving producer market featuring more than 80 stalls.

Website: **www.regionalflavours.com.au**

August – The Royal Queensland Show (The Ekka)

Usually in the second and third week of August the 'Ekka-xibition' is Queensland's single biggest event – an agricultural show that attracts 400,000 people to the **Brisbane Showgrounds** (page 58) to see 21,000 entrants vie for competition prizes in a carnival atmosphere.

Website: **www.ekka.com.au**

September – The Brisbane Festival

Taking up most of the year's ninth month the Brisbane Festival is a pretext for showcasing a whole bunch of live shows, music performances, comedy, dance, theater, film, opera and other performing and fine arts events that can't be crammed in at any other time of the year.

The Brisbane Festival rounds off its three-week-long celebration with Sunsuper Riverfire, a mega fireworks display over the river in the CBD.

Website: **www.brisbanefestival.com.au**

October – Oktoberfest

Unlike Munich's Oktoberfest that starts in September, Brisbane's Oktoberfest actually happens over two weekends in its eponymous month. So much to see, do and experience at Brisbane Showgrounds – easily reached with a short train ride from Central to Exhibition Station – and all of it so German, with maybe a touch of Austrian and Swiss …

Website: **www.oktoberfestbrisbane.com.au**

Late October/Early November – The Good Food and Wine Show

After visiting Melbourne, Perth, Adelaide and Sydney the show ends its tour in Brisbane. Here's your pretext to sample food and beverages that you normally wouldn't and your chance to hob-nob with a celebrity chef or two.

Website: **www.goodfoodshow.com.au**

October/November – Brisbane International Film Festival

Featuring all styles and genres including world cinema, documentaries, retrospectives, experimental work, thrillers, animation, children's films and much more.

Website: **www.biff.com.au**

December – Woodford Folk Festival

Woodford folk festival attracts around 130,000 people each year from far and wide to ring in the new year on a rural property north of the **Sunshine Coast** (page 104) town of Woodford. The festival takes place over six nights from 27 December and features local and international musical acts as well as circus, cabaret, street performers and workshops.

Website: **www.woodfordfolkfestival.com**

Eateries and Drinkeries

Obviously, you're going to have to eat and drink at some point and where and what will depend on your whims, moods and, literally, your tastes. You can find food from virtually anywhere in the world in Brisbane, with different cultural communities established and thriving across the city.

Naturally, restaurants, cafes, wine bars, pubs and other establishments often change their menus and even their opening times depending on season and time of the year, so we can only offer an approximate idea of highly recommended venues and it's best to check their websites for their current status.

Breakfast and Brunch

Anouk

212 Given Terrace, Paddington 4064
Open: 6.30 am to 3.00 pm, seven days.
Phone: 07 3367 8663
Website: **www.anoukcafe.com**
Known for: Great all-day breakfast cafe in Paddington, within
an easy stroll of Empire Revival (167 Latrobe Terrace), a huge
antiques emporium. Buzzy, restyled old apothecary with original
bay windows and exposed brick walls.

Billykart Kitchen

1 Eric Crescent, Annerley 4103
Open: 6.30 am to 3.00 pm then 5.30 pm to 10.00 pm Wednesday
to Sunday
Phone: 07 3392 9275
Website: **www.billykart.com.au**
Known for: TV chef Ben O'Donoghue's seasonal menu in a sleek
cafe that was once a corner store, with wood floors and retro
coffee machine.

The Gunshop Café

53 Mollison St, West End 4101
Open: 7.00 am to 3.00 pm, seven days.
Phone: 07 3844 2241
Website: **www.thegunshopcafe.com**
Known for: Vibrant spot with brick walls, a leafy courtyard and
rooftop beehives, serving creative breakfasts and market
specials.

Campos Coffee Long Island

18 Longland Street, Newstead 4006

Open: 6.00 am to 5.00 pm Monday to Friday, 7.00 am to 5.00 pm
  weekends.

Phone: 07 3252 3612

Website: **www.camposcoffee.com**

Known for: Being casual and big enough for kids and groups.

Food with a View and Fine Dining

1889 Enoteca

10–12 Logan Road, Woolloongabba 4101

Open for lunch noon to 2.30 pm Tuesday to Friday and Sunday
  and for dinner 6.00 pm to late Tuesday to Saturday.

Phone: 07 3392 4315

Website: **www.1889enoteca.com.au**

Known for: A modern Roman-style Italian restaurant serving
  handmade pasta and organic wine in a heritage-listed building.

Bacchus

Rydges Hotel, corner Grey and Glenelg Streets, South Bank 4101

Open for breakfast from 6.00 am to 10.00 am seven days; for
  lunch from 2.30 pm to 4.30 pm Tuesday to Friday and from
  1.30 pm to 4.30 pm weekends; for dinner from 5.30 pm to late
  Tuesday to Saturday.

Phone: 07 3364 0837

Website: bacchussouthbank.com.au

Known for: Modern Australian fine dining, plus clever cocktails,
  in a glamorous restaurant and bar. High tea also available.

Patina at Customs House

399 Queen Street, Brisbane City 4000

Open for lunch noon to 4.00 pm Monday to Saturday, for dinner from 6.00 pm to late Tuesday to Saturday and for brunch 9.30 am to 4.00 pm Sunday.

Phone: 07 3365 8999

Website: **www.patinarestaurant.com.au**

Known for: A chic contemporary Australian restaurant in a grand heritage-listed building with a terrace overlooking the river.

Grappino Italian

226 Given Terrace, Paddington 4064

Open: for lunch noon to 4.00 pm Thursday and Friday and for dinner 5.00 pm to 10.00 pm Tuesday to Saturday.

Phone: 07 3367 0033

Website: **www.grappino.com.au**

Known for: Low-key ambience. Traditional Italian dishes in an informal room hung with movie posters and chalkboards.

Greca

Howard Smith Wharves, 3/5 Boundary Street, Brisbane City 4000

Open: noon to 11.00 pm seven days.

Phone: 07 3839 1203

Website: **www.greca.com.au**

Known for: All-day dining beneath the Story Bridge with contemporary Greek share plates in a relaxed, casual atmosphere, outdoor seating and vegetarian options.

Happy Boy

East Street (between Wickham Street and Ann Street),
Fortitude Valley 4006

Open for lunch 11.30 am to 2.00 pm Tuesday to Saturday and for
dinner 5.30 pm to 8.30 pm Sunday, Tuesday and Wednesday, to
9.30 pm Thursday, Friday and Saturday.

Phone: 0413 246 890

Website: **www.happyboy.com.au**

Known for: Hip Fortitude Valley venue serving authentic Chinese
BBQ, noodles and seafood, with an extensive wine list. Dine
under fairy lights and there's a large outdoor deck.

Hellenika at The Calile

Level 1/48 James Street, Fortitude Valley 4006

Open: 6.30 am to midnight, seven days.

Phone: 07 3252 2060

Website: **www.hellenika.com.au**

Known for: Great Greek food in a contemporary, light venue with
poolside dining and great cocktails.

Honto

23 Alden Street, Fortitude Valley 4006

Open: 5.30 pm to late Tuesday to Saturday.

Phone: 07 3193 7392

Website: **www.honto.com.au**

Known for: Dark and moody space with great Japanese food,
Japanese whiskey and sake. Very laid back and at the 'gritty end'
of The Valley.

La Cache à Vín

215 Wharf St, Spring Hill 4000

Open: noon to 11.00 pm Monday to Friday.

Phone: 07 3924 0501

Website: **www.lacacheavin.com.au**

Known for: Being one of the best restaurants in Brisbane. This Lyonnaise-style French restaurant with a huge French wine list is so good it doesn't even have to open on weekends to stay in business, so it doesn't!

La Vue Waterfront Restaurant

1/501 Queen Street, Brisbane City 4000

Open for lunch 11.30 am to 3.00 pm Friday and for dinner 5.30 pm to 11.00 pm, seven days.

Phone: 07 3831 1400

Website: **www.lavuerestaurant.com.au**

Known for: Sophisticated French-inspired modern Australian in a light-filled dining room overlooking the river.

Sono Japanese Restaurant Portside Wharf

39 Hercules Street, Hamilton 4007

Open for lunch noon to 2.30 pm Wednesday to Sunday, dinner 6.00 pm to late Tuesday to Sunday.

Phone: 07 3268 6655

Website: **www.sonorestaurant.com.au**

Known for: Modern, creative Japanese food, a teppanyaki bar and a sake tasting menu in a refined, riverfront space.

Urbane Restaurant

181 Mary Street, Brisbane City 4001

Open 6.00 pm to midnight Thursday, Friday and Saturday.

Phone: 07 3229 2271

Website: **www.urbanerestaurant.com**

Known for: Being a stylish dining space screened by bronze mesh and offering creative degustation only menus with global influences.

Bar and Pub Dining and Gastropubs

Sometimes you just want to have a nice place to sit down and eat without any formality and this is where bar and pub dining comes into its own. 'Gastropub' is a word that combines the idea of gastronomy and pub. They're venues in which the eaties are as important as the drinkies – one up from a cafe but not quite fine dining. The venues below are reputed to be wonderful places to eat and usually lend themselves to a relaxed, casual atmosphere. As usual, contact the venue to check if you need to book in order to avoid disappointment.

Bar Alto

119 Lamington Street, New Farm 4005

Phone: 07 3358 1063

Website: **www.baralto.com.au**

Open: 11.30 am to late Tuesday to Sunday.

Known for: Located in the **Brisbane Powerhouse** (page 54) with views of the river and a modern Italian menu.

Beccofino

10 Vernon Terrace, Teneriffe 4005

Phone: 07 3666 0207

Website: **www.beccofino.com.au**

Open: 5.30 pm to late Tuesday to Saturday, noon to 9.00 pm
Sunday.

Known for: Authentic Italian woodfired thin-crust pizzas and
home-style Italian favorites

Buffalo Bar

169 Mary Street, Brisbane City 4000

Phone: 07 3051 7620

Website: **www.buffalobar.com.au**

Open: 11.30 am to 10.00 pm Sunday to Thursday, to 11.00 pm
Friday and Saturday.

Known for: An American sports bar featuring classics like burgers,
hotdogs and Buffalo wings as well as a beer garden with craft
beers and Hank's Lounge for small-batch whiskey.

Embassy Craft Beer Bar

214 Elizabeth Street, Brisbane City 4000

Phone: 07 3221 7616

Website: **www.embassybar.com.au**

Open: 11.00 am to 10.00 pm Monday to Thursday and Saturday,
11.00 am to 12.00 am Friday.

Known for: Heritage-listed, exposed brick interiors, a big range of
craft beers, an updated hearty pub menu and live music.

Julius Pizzeria

77 Grey Street, South Brisbane 4101

Phone: 07 3844 2655

Website: **www.juliuspizzeria.com.au**

Open: noon to late Tuesday to Sunday.

Known for: Woodfired pizza, Italian favorites and a wide range of Italian wine and beer in an industrial-chic space in the cultural precinct. Bookings generally only for early sittings.

Norman Hotel

102 Ipswich Road, Woolloongabba 4102

Phone: 07 3391 5022

Website: **www.normanhotel.com.au**

Open for lunch from 11.30 am seven days, and for dinner from 5.30 pm to 9.00 pm seven days (to 9.30 pm Friday and Saturday).

Known for: Iconic steakhouse with a meat cabinet – known as 'Brisbane's worst vegetarian restaurant'! Family friendly.

Regatta Hotel

543 Coronation Drive, Toowong 4066

Phone: 07 3051 7617

Website: **www.regattahotel.com.au**

Open: 11.00 am to 10.00 pm Sunday to Friday, to 11.00 pm Saturday.

Known for: Grand Victorian hotel located on the Brisbane River – it has a ferry terminal right outside! **The Boatshed** restaurant is family-friendly with a kids' menu, stylish yet comfortable decor, and dry-aged steaks cooked on the flame grill.

The Alliance Hotel

320 Boundary Street, Spring Hill 4000

Phone: 07 3839 0169

Website: **www.thealliancehotel.com.au**

Open for dinner daily from 5.30 pm to 8.30 pm Sunday to Thursday, to 9.00 pm Friday and Saturday.

Known for: One of Brisbane's oldest pubs had a stylish makeover and the bistro features refined upmarket pub food.

Coffee, Cake and the Occasional Other

Brew Café and Wine Bar

Lower, Burnett Lane, Brisbane City 4000

Phone: 07 3211 4242

Website: **www.brewcafewinebar.com.au**

Open 7.00 am to late Monday to Friday, 8.00 am to late Saturday and Sunday.

Known for: Cafe and wine bar hidden down a laneway. We couldn't decide where to put this one, so we erred on the side of 'coffee'.

Bunker Coffee

21 Railway Terrace, Milton 4064

Phone: 0422 124 767

Website: **www.bunkercoffee.com.au**

Open 6.00 am to 3.30 pm Monday to Friday.

Known for: Its unique location in an old World War II air raid shelter covered in vines, specialty coffee and a dozen flavors of hot chocolate.

Cartel Coffee

Ground Floor, 102 Adelaide Street, Brisbane City 4001

Phone: 0421 779 896

Website: **www.facebook.com/The.Cartel.Coffee**

Open 6.30 am to 4.00 pm Monday to Friday, 7.30 am to 4.00 pm Saturday, 9.00 am to 3.00 pm Sunday.

Known for: Roasting their own organic, fair trade coffee, fast and friendly service.

Duce & Co

271 Edward Street, Brisbane City 4000

Phone: 0490 084 842

Website: **www.facebook.com/duceandco**

Open 6.30 am to 4.00 pm Monday to Friday.

Known for: Cozy downstairs coffee nook near Central Station. Participates in the 'pay it forward' scheme.

Edward Specialty Coffee

25/275 Edward Street, Brisbane City 4000

Phone: 0429 160 435

Website: **www.edwardspecialtycoffee.com**

Open 6.00 am to 4.00 pm Monday to Friday.

Known for: Unique espresso varieties in the historic Anzac Square Arcade near Central Station.

John Mills Himself

40 Charlotte St, Brisbane City 4000

Phone: 0434 064 349

Website: **www.johnmillshimself.com.au**

Open 6.30 am to 3.30 pm Monday to Friday.

Known for: Turns into a hip bar in the evenings. Owned and operated by the same team as **Bunker Coffee** (and also has the hot chocolates). Prides itself on its ethical practices.

LAB Specialty Coffee Co.

79 Albert Street, Brisbane City 4000

Phone: 07 3211 2484

Website: **www.facebook.com/streetlabspecialtycoffee**

Open 7.00 am to 3.00 pm Monday to Friday.

Known for: Specialty coffee with a focus on black coffee (including two- and three-day brews).

Marchetti Cafe

202 Edward Street, Brisbane City 4000

Phone: 07 3003 1344.

Website: **www.marchetticafe.com**

Open 7.00 am to 4.00 pm Monday to Thursday, 7.00 am to 8.00 pm Friday, 8.00 am to 4.00 pm Saturday, 9.00 am to 4.00 pm Sunday.

Known for: Stylish Italian cafe and wine bar in the Tattersall's Arcade.

Pablo & Rusty's Coffee Roasters

200 Mary Street, Brisbane City 4000

Phone: 07 3236 4525

Website: **www.pabloandrustys.com.au**

Open 6.30 am to 3.30 pm Monday to Friday.

Known for: Sleek modern space with a full food menu, including delicious gluten free treats. Cards only – no cash!

Strauss

189–191 Elizabeth Street, Brisbane City 4002

Phone: 07 3236 5232

Website: **www.straussfd.com**

Open 6.30 am to 3.00 pm Monday to Friday.

Known for: Cozy, exposed brick laneway cafe with a full food menu. Turns into a bar Wednesday to Friday evenings.

High Tea

There's nothing quite like sitting down for several hours at a nice establishment, sipping perfectly steeped tea and noshing on delicate scones, cakes and tiny sandwiches with the crusts cut off. Welcome to the world of high tea. High tea is very popular in Brisbane with a number of cafes and restaurants vying for your attention. We strongly recommend making a booking so that you're not disappointed.

Depending on where you go high tea can happen either throughout the week or only on weekends. It's generally served after lunch, from about 3.00 pm, but some venues prefer to serve it earlier, virtually as a substitute for brunch or lunch, from as early as 10.00 am. High tea is also often served with a champagne option.

Depending on the venues, high tea varies in tone from traditional to more modern. Prices generally hover at around the $45 to $75 mark depending on the level of swank. Use the price and the way the website looks as a guideline of how formally you'll have to attire yourself. Believe us when we tell you that you'll enjoy high tea much more if you dress up for some venues and make it an event. This is not to say that high tea isn't kid friendly, as some venues cater for them too. Shingle Inn, for example, has a 'Teddy Bear High Tea' option.

You'll need to budget around an hour and a half to two hours on top of your travel time because rushing completely defeats the purpose of high tea.

Here is a collection of some of the best high teas available in the city.

Customs House

399 Queen Street, Brisbane
Phone: 07 3365 8999
Website: **www.customshouse.com.au/high-tea**

Dello Mano (of the Hand) at the Tattersall's Arcade

215 Queen Street, Brisbane 4000
Phone: 07 3210 1168
Website: **www.dellomano.com.au/pages/**
  visit-dello-mano-at-tattersalls-arcade
Dello Mano is particularly famous for its range of boutique brownies. They serve 'Arcadian' and 'Chocolate Queen' high teas on weekends only.

Keri Craig Emporium Fashion Cafe

Lower Level Brisbane Arcade, 160 Queen Street Mall, Brisbane 4000

Phone: 07 3211 2797

Website: **www.kericraig.com.au**

Ovolo Inchcolm Hotel

73 Wickham Terrace, Spring Hill 4000

Phone: 07 3226 888

Website: It's long so Google it or call.

The Ovolo Rock 'n' Roll High Teas are another tradition breaker with options named after songs – 'Like a Virgin', 'Start Me Up', 'Welcome to the Jungle' and 'The Final Countdown'. Saturday afternoons only.

Room with Roses

Gallery Level Brisbane Arcade, 160 Queen Street Mall, Brisbane 4000

Phone: 07 3229 7050

Website: **www.roomwithroses.com.au**

Shingle Inn City Hall

King George Square, Brisbane 4000

Phone: 07 3210 2904

Website: **www.shingleinncityhall.com/high-tea**

Very kid friendly – for children under 12 the Teddy Bear High Tea costs $15.50 per child and includes ham and cheese sandwiches, fairy bread, mini sausage rolls and teddy bear biscuits.

Sofitel Brisbane City

249 Turbot Street, Brisbane 4000

Phone: 07 3835 3535

Website: **www.sofitelbrisbane.com.au** browse to the 'restaurants and bars' menu then scroll down to 'high tea'

High tea at the Sofitel is served from 11.00 am at both the 30th floor Club Millésime Lounge (to 3.00 pm) or in the 1960s inspired Cuvee Lounge Bar (to 4.00 pm), seven days.

Stamford Plaza

39 Edward Street, Brisbane 4000

Phone: 07 3221 1999

Website: **www.stamford.com.au/spb/restaurant--bar/ brisbane-high-tea**

The Stamford go out of their way with their high teas, with a number of options – Spirit of Queensland Lobby High Tea, Chocolate High Tea Buffet, Guilt-Free High Tea (low-fat, low-sugar). There's even a takeaway high tea for those who want to have an elegant picnic elsewhere, which you can pick up from The Brasserie on the River.

W Hotel

81 North Quay, Brisbane 4000

Phone: 07 3556 8888

Website: **www.deals.marriott.com.au/w-hotels-resorts/australia/qld/ brisbane/brisbanehightea**

Serves an entirely non-traditional high tea, the High Tea of Aus, which features reimagined Australian classics like the meat pie, lamington and Milo in a glamorous, funky setting.

Food Experiences You Have to Try

Brisbane Lookout

If you're going to **Mount Coot-tha** (page 28) and you're in no hurry to rush back to the CBD, consider enjoying the sensation while you have a light meal at the **Kuta Café** or the **Summit Restaurant and Bar**. The Summit also does high teas on Sundays.

Phone: 07 3369 9922

Websites: **www.brisbanelookout.com/kuta-cafe**;
   www.brisbanelookout.com/summit-restaurant-and-bar

The Curated Plate

Even though it only happens once a year in August and it's on the Sunshine Coast, The Curated Plate is considered by many to be one of the best food festivals around, featuring the best chefs from Australia and around the world, in the picturesque surrounds of a region famed for its vibrant produce.

Website: **www.thecuratedplate.com.au/sunshine-coast**

Eat Street Northshore

Imagine 180 shipping containers converted into a space where over 70 vendors can tempt you with dishes from all over the world catering to all sorts of preferences and dietary restrictions. Its creators say that there's nowhere else in the world quite like it, and they're right. Highlights of Eat Street include, but are by no means limited to: Home Brewed Ginger Beer, Miss Flossy Lemonade, Mocktail Madness, Don't Worry Eat Curry, Hungarian Langos, WOW Gourmet Sausages. And it's not all just about food and drink. You can get temporary henna tattoos at Henna Boutique, you can make your own candles and get yourself a dream catcher at The Trinket Box. Entry costs $3 per person, children 12 and under FREE!

Address: 221D MacArthur Ave, Hamilton 4007

Phone: 0428 485 242

Website: **www.eatstreetnorthshore.com.au/eat_and_drink**

Open: from 4.00 pm to 10.00 pm Friday and Saturday and noon to 8.00 pm Sunday.

How to get there: From Central walk to Adelaide Street stop 23 near David Jones department store. Take bus 300 to Nudgee Road near Allen Street, stop 29 Hamilton. From there, walk south along Remora Road until you reach Macarthur Avenue then turn left (east) along MacArthur Avenue. Keep walking. It's a 1.5-kilometer (1 mile) walk so it'll take you about 20 minutes, after which you'll have earned your meal. Alternatively, take a ferry to Northshore Hamilton ferry terminal and you'll be walking west for only about 700 meters (½ mile), so you won't be able to justify eating as much.

Golden Pig Cooking Class

For those who are inclined to the creative side of cookery, who need a pretext to upgrade their skills, and who like to feel that they can justify their holiday if they come out of it a 'better person', consider doing a cooking class at the Golden Pig. Chef Katrina Ryan (ex-Rockpool and Spirit House) offers a nice little selection of culinary educational options several times a week. Katrina describes them as very 'hands on' so you're not just sitting back watching her cook, you're actually doing it.

Examples include, but are not limited to: Thai Seafood, Pig Butchery, A Taste of Vietnam, Modern Italian, French Bistro, Sourdough and Bread, Moroccan and More, Mexican Street Food, Beer, Birds, Beef and Barbecue, Kitchen Essentials, Pastry Essentials, Vegan Essentials, Little Tastes of Spain, Dessert Masterclass … we could go on, but you get the drift.

Address: 38 Ross Street, Newstead 4006

Phone: 07 3666 0884

Website: **www.goldenpig.com.au**

How to get there: From Central take the train to Bowen Hills Station, then go a little way north along Abbotsford Road, turn right (east) at Folkstone Street until you get to the roundabout. Go north-east up Ross Street (the soft left, not the hard left, that's Edmondstone Road, you don't want that one) for one block and you're there.

Open: Classes generally start at 9.00 am, 10.00 am or 2.00 pm depending on the day.

Time budget: Allow four hours per class.

How much? Most classes are $165, couples are $200 and there's a charcuterie class that's $235 because of the cost of the ingredients. You'll need to book and you can do so online where you can browse classes, dates and times.

While you're in the area: The fully licensed restaurant is open for lunch on Friday and for dinner from 5.30 pm from Tuesday to Saturday.

Drinks with a View and the Best Rooftop Bars

Dandy's Rooftop Bar

71–73 Melbourne Street, South Brisbane 4101

Phone: 07 3844 2883

Website: **www.thefox.com.au**

Open Thursday 5.00 pm to late, Friday 4.00 pm to late, Saturday and Sunday 2.00 pm to late.

Known for: Fun venue, part of the iconic Fox Hotel, with cocktails and pizzas, live jazz on Thursday evenings and DJs on Sundays.

Eagles Nest

21 Lambert Street, Kangaroo Point 4169

Phone: 1800 088 388

Website: **www.eaglesnestbrisbane.com.au**

Open 3.00 pm to 11.00 pm Fridays and 3.00 pm to 7.00 pm Sundays.

Known for: Stylish 12th floor bar in The Point hotel with tapas menu, cocktails, champagne and live music.

Eleven Rooftop Bar

757 Ann Street, Fortitude Valley 4006

Phone: 07 3067 7447

Website: **www.elevenrooftopbar.com.au**

Open for coffee from 8.30 am to 12.00 pm Tuesday to Friday, from noon to 12.00 am Tuesday to Thursday and Sunday and from noon to 3.00 am Saturday.

Known for: Cool and stylish with lounge seating and a large menu. On weekends it has an up-market party atmosphere.

Elixir Rooftop Bar

646 Ann Street, Brisbane City 4006

Phone: 07 3363 5599

Website: **www.elixirrooftop.com.au**

Open 4.00 pm to late Monday, Thursday and Friday and 1.00 pm to late Saturday and Sunday.

Known for: Cocktails and tapas with sophisticated wooden decor and greenery and a trendy crowd.

Sazerac Bar

Level 30/99 Mary Street, Brisbane City 4000 (within Four Points by Sheraton Brisbane)

Phone: 07 3164 4000

Website: **www.sazeracbarbrisbane.com**

Open 4.00 pm to late Wednesday to Saturday.

Known for: Stylish bar on level 30 with craft beers, cocktails and bar bites.

Sixteen Antlers

Level 16, Pullman & Mercure Hotel, corner of Ann and Roma Streets, Brisbane City 4000

Phone: 0466 463 742

Website: **www.sixteenantlers.com.au**

Open 3.00 pm to late Tuesday to Thursday, 2.00 pm to late Friday and Saturday.

Known for: Relaxed rooftop lounge bar with craft beer, cocktails and a tapas menu, DJs on Friday and Saturday evenings.

Soleil Pool Bar

Glenelg Street, South Brisbane 4101 (within Rydges South Bank hotel)

Phone: 07 3364 0838

Website: **www.soleilpoolbar.com.au**

Open from noon to late seven days.

Known for: Chic poolside bar with interesting cocktails and punches as well as beer and wine, DJs and live music on weekends.

The Stock Exchange Hotel

131 Edward Street, Brisbane City 4000

Phone: 07 3229 3522

Website: **www.stockexchangehotel.com.au**

Open 11.00 am to late Monday to Wednesday, 11.00 am to 3.00 am Thursday and Friday, noon to 3.00 pm Saturday and Sunday.

Known for: A garden oasis with a stylish bistro menu

Wine, spirits and cocktails

Baedeker Wine Bar

111 Constance Street, Fortitude Valley 4006

Phone: 07 3257 4482

Website: **www.baedeker.com.au**

Open from 4.00 pm to late Thursday, 12.00 pm to late Friday and 2.00 pm to late Saturday.

Known for: Elegant 1930s style wine room and bar with whiskey and cocktails and a small plates menu to match.

The Cloakroom Bar

215 Elizabeth Street, Brisbane City 4000

Phone: 07 3210 1515

Website: **www.cloakroombar.co** (There's one in Montreal too so don't get them mixed up!)

Open 5.00 pm to 12.00 am Tuesday to Saturday.

Known for: Innovative, dimly lit bespoke bar (you may be asked about your preferences and what you usually like to drink) creating innovative cocktails. The entrance is from a fire escape down an alleyway.

CRU Bar and Cellar

1/22 James Street, Fortitude Valley 4006

Phone: 07 3252 2400

Website: **www.crubar.com**

Open 11.00 am to late seven days.

Known for: Bright and stylish wine bar and shop with a full food menu.

Grape Therapy Wine Merchants and Drinking Den

471 Adelaide Street, Brisbane City 4000

Phone: 07 3102 7213

Website: **www.grapetherapy.com.au**

Open 4.00 pm to late seven days.

Known for: Intimate underground wine bar with an old-world feel and cheese and charcuterie boards to pair with the wine. You can buy the wine to take home.

The Gresham Bar

308 Queen Street, Brisbane City 4000

Phone: 0437 360 158

Website: **www.thegresham.com.au**

Open 7.00 am to 3.00 am Monday to Friday, noon to 3.00 am Saturday, 4.00 pm to 3.00 am Sunday.

Known for: Vintage decor in a heritage-listed Victorian sandstone pub with a focus on whiskey (more than 200!), rum and other spirits.

La Lune Wine Co

44 Fish Lane, South Brisbane 4101

Phone: 07 3255 0010

Website: **www.lalunewineco.com.au**

Open 4.00 pm to 11.00 pm Tuesday to Thursday, noon to 12.00 am Friday and Saturday, noon to 11.00 pm Sunday.

Known for: Stylish, sophisticated wine bar with European-style menu.

The Laneway

181 Mary Street, Brisbane City 4001

Phone: 07 3229 3686

Website: **www.theeuro.com.au/laneway**

Open Thursday 5.00 pm to late, Friday noon to late,
Saturday 6.00 pm to late.

Known for: Intimate cocktail bar with a laneway entry
(hence the name) and gourmet bar food and share plates.

Lychee Lounge

2/94 Boundary Street, West End 4101

Phone: 0411 888 561

Website: **www.lycheelounge.com.au**

Open 4.30 pm to late Wednesday to Sunday.

Known for: Oriental-style decor and a tapas menu.

Maker

9 Fish Lane, South Brisbane 4101

Phone: 07 3844 1222

Website: No website

Open 4.00 pm to 12.00 am Tuesday to Sunday.

Known for: A creative cocktail list using native ingredients.

Moo Moo The Wine Bar and Grill

The Port Office Building, Stamford Plaza, 39 Edward Street,
Brisbane City 4000

Phone: 07 3236 4500

Website: **www.moomoorestaurant.com**

Open noon to 3.00 pm then 5.30 pm to late seven days.

Known for: Steak restaurant and wine bar.

Mr Chester Wine Bar

2/850 Ann Street, Fortitude Valley 4006

Phone: No phone.

Website: **www.mrchesterwine.com**

Open from noon to late Tuesday to Saturday and 4.00 pm to late Sunday; dinner from 5.30 pm to late.

Known for: Wine bar and wine shop focused on smaller boutique producers. Card only – no cash!

Mr and Mrs G Riverbar

1 Eagle Street (in the Eagle Street Pier), Brisbane City 4000

Phone: 07 3221 7001

Website: **www.mrandmrsg.com.au**

Open noon to late Wednesday to Friday and Sunday, 3.00 pm to late Monday, Tuesday and Saturday.

Known for: Bright and stylish cocktail bar with a tapas menu and riverside views.

Proud Henry Wine Bar and Ginoteca

153 Wickham Street, Brisbane City 4006

Phone: 07 3102 1237

Website: **www.proudhenry.com.au**

Open noon to late Monday to Friday, 4.00 pm to late Saturday.

Known for: Featuring 250 artisan gins and wines from around the world you can also buy wine to take away and they host live acoustic music.

Russell Street Wine Bar

Russell Street, South Brisbane 4101
(within the Queensland Performing Arts Centre)
Phone: 07 3840 7444
Website: **www.qpac.com.au/eat-drink/russell-street-wine-bar**
Open when there's a show on – generally 5.30 pm to 10.00 pm
   Thursday to Saturday.
Known for: Stylish wine bar with tapas, cheese and charcuterie and
views of South Bank.

Super Whatnot

48 Burnett Lane, Brisbane City 4000
Phone: 07 3210 2343
Website: **www.superwhatnot.com**
Open 3.00 pm to 12.00 am Monday to Thursday and Saturday,
   noon to 12.00 am Friday.
Known for: Funky laneway bar with interesting wines, craft beers
   and DJs. Look out for the big 'S' – there's no sign!

The Silver Fox Wine Bar

2 Edward Street, Brisbane City 4000
Phone: 07 3151 7522
Website: **www.silverfoxwinebar.com.au**
Open 4.00 pm to 12.00 am Tuesday to Saturday.
Known for: Moody and sophisticated wine bar near the **Brisbane
   City Botanic Gardens** (page 50) with chandeliers and lounge
   seating and a menu of cheese and charcuterie.

The Valley Wine Bar

171 Alfred Street, Fortitude Valley 4006

Phone: 07 3252 2224

Website: **www.thevalleywinebar.com**

Open 3.00 pm to 9.00 pm Sunday and Tuesday, noon to 11.00 pm
  Wednesday to Saturday.

Known for: Wine shop and bar with a huge wine list including 20
  wines by the glass, accompanied by wine-friendly snacks and
  small plates.

Breweries

Brews Brothers Microbrewery

31 Wellington Road, East Brisbane 4169

Phone: 07 3891 3050

Website: **www.brewsbrothers.com.au**

Open noon to 6.00 pm Wednesday, noon to 8.00 pm Thursday,
  noon to 7.00 pm Friday, 9.00 am to 4.00 pm Saturday, 10.00 am
  to 2.00 pm Sunday.

Brisbane Brewing Co

124 Boundary Street, West End 4101

Phone: 07 3891 1011

Website: **www.brisbanebrewing.com.au**

Open 4.00 pm to late Monday to Thursday, 11.00 am to late
  Friday to Sunday.

The Catchment Brewing Co

150 Boundary Street, West End 4101
Phone: 07 3846 1701
Website: **www.catchmentbrewingco.com.au**
Open 4.00 pm to 10.00 pm Tuesday and Wednesday, noon to
12.00 am Thursday, noon to 1.00 am Friday and Saturday,
noon to 10.00 pm Sunday.

Felons Brewing Co

5 Boundary Street, Brisbane City 4000
(within the Howard Smith Wharves district)
Phone: 07 3188 9090
Website: **www.felonsbrewingco.com.au**
Open 11.00 am to late seven days.

Green Beacon Brewing Co.

26 Helen Street, Teneriffe 4005
Phone: 07 3257 3565
Website: **www.greenbeacon.com.au**
Open noon to late seven days.

Newstead Brewing Co

67 Castlemaine Street, Milton 4064
Phone: 07 3367 0490
Website: **www.newsteadbrewing.com.au**
Open 10.00 am to late seven days.

Range Brewing

4 Byres Street, Newstead 4006

Phone: 07 3310 4456

Website: **www.rangebrewing.com**

Open 4.00 pm to 7.00 pm Wednesday, 4.00 pm to 10.00 pm Thursday, noon to late Friday and Saturday and noon to 10.00 pm Sunday.

XXXX Brewery Tours

No beer lover's visit to Brisbane would be complete without taking a tour of the XXXX Brewery.

Address: Level 1, corner of Black and Paten Streets, Milton 4064

Phone: 07 3361 7597

Website: **xxxx.com.au**

Open: The brewery itself is open from 10.00 am to 9.00 pm.

Tour times: Tuesday, Thursday and Friday at 11.00 am, 1.00 pm– 3.00 pm and 5.00 pm. Saturday first tour at 11.00 am and then every 30 minutes thereafter until 2.00 pm. Then 3.00 pm and 5.00 pm. Closed Sunday, Monday and Wednesday but call to enquire for group bookings.

How Much? Adults $32, children $18.

The tours take approximately 90 minutes and conclude with a beer-tasting session with your tour guide (for the adults only, obviously, kids have to make do with soft drink). Please ensure you are wearing fully enclosed flat shoes, have not consumed any alcohol prior to the tour and have government proof of ID with you. The XXXX Brewery Tours have many steps and cannot accommodate guests with walking aids such as crutches and wheelchairs.

First published in 2019 by New Holland Publishers
Sydney • Auckland

Level 1, 178 Fox Valley Road, Wahroonga, NSW 2076, Australia
5/39 Woodside Ave, Northcote, Auckland 0627, New Zealand

newhollandpublishers.com

A record of this book is held at the National Library of Australia.

ISBN 9781760791407

Group Managing Director: Fiona Schultz
Author: Xavier Waterkeyn
Project Editor: Liz Hardy
Designer: Andrew Davies
Production Director: Arlene Gippert
Printer: Toppan Leefung Printing Limited

10 9 8 7 6 5 4 3 2 1

Keep up with New Holland Publishers:
 NewHollandPublishers
 @newhollandpublishers